Profiles of
Shingo Prize-Winning Organizations

Management Accounting in Support of Manufacturing Excellence

by

Richard L. Jenson, Ph.D., CPA
James W. Brackner, Ph.D., CMA, CPA
Clifford R. Skousen, Ph. D., CMA, CPA

A research report carried out on behalf of
The IMA Foundation for Applied Research, Inc.
Institute of Management Accountants
Montvale, New Jersey

Published by
The IMA Foundation for Applied Research, Inc.
10 Paragon Drive
Montvale, NJ 07645-1760

♻ Printed on recycled paper

The IMA Foundation for Applied Research, Inc. (FAR) is the research affiliate of the Institute of Management Accountants. The mission of the Foundation is to develop and disseminate timely management accounting research findings that can be applied to current and emerging business issues.

Claire Barth, editor

Copyright © 1996 by The IMA Foundation for Applied Research, Inc.
All rights reserved.
IMA Publication Number 239-96311
ISBN 0-86641-248-4

Foreword

Our culture rewards outstanding performance. We are motivated by the value others place on what we do. We are inspired to do more by what others have achieved. This passion for performance recognition is well articulated by Richard Jenson, James Brackner, and Clifford Skousen in their research study, *Management Accounting in Support of Manufacturing Excellence: Profiles of Award-winning Organizations*, sponsored by The IMA Foundation for Applied Research, Inc. (FAR).

The ability to manage the performance recognition process for the good of the enterprise is an indicator of how well management performs as commitments to build cross-functional teams are translated into bottom-line results. The experiences of eight Shingo Award winners in achieving excellence have common characteristics. The one that stands out is the role a rich base of knowledge played in attaining their success. The tools and techniques that make up this knowledge are collectively known as *management accounting*.

Employees properly trained, empowered by management, and committed to excellence make the difference between winning and losing the competitive race. The exceptional winners are those whose employees exhibit an alignment between personal values and the goals of the enterprise. Operational managers with applied management accounting know-how coupled with creative thinking make an unbeatable combination. Read the cases and see for yourself what the elements were that helped these companies achieve the coveted award.

Readers are encouraged to obtain the latest Shingo Prize Application Guidelines. It contains useful criteria that can be used to compare your business manufacturing strategy with the best practices. You can use the material as a self-assessment tool to see if you would qualify.

FAR trustees are pleased to add these findings to a growing collection of FAR-sponsored field studies conducted by highly qualified researchers. An annotated list of recent titles issued by FAR can be found on the back page of this monograph. Among them is *Management Accounting Issues in Cellular Manufacturing and Focused-Factory Systems*; the principles of cellular manufacturing are referenced in this study. FAR's intent is to show the corporate community that knowledge learned from others can be replicated. Success awaits those who manage the process wisely.

Guidance in the preparation of this report was generously provided by the IMA Project Committee formed when IMA's research activities were under the oversight of the Committee on Research (1992-1993):

> Ray Vander Weele, CMA, *Chair*
> Merrill Lynch
> Grand Rapids, Michigan

Arjan T. Sadhwani	Lloyd O. Schatschneider
University of Akron	Lerner Publications Company
Akron, Ohio	Minneapolis, Minnesota

This report reflects the views of the researchers and not necessarily those of the FAR trustees or the Project Committee.

> Julian M. Freedman, CMA, CPA, CPIM
> *Senior Director of Research*
> The IMA Foundation for Applied Research, Inc.

The Shingo Prize Application Guidelines can be obtained by contacting:

The Shingo Prize for Excellence in Manufacturing
College of Business
Utah State University
Logan, UT 84322-3521

(801) 797-2279
Fax: (801) 797-3440

Preface

Dramatic changes have taken place in manufacturing throughout the world during the last two decades. Increased international competition to market products has forced companies to reexamine their manufacturing methods and product designs so they can remain competitive in a global market. American companies have faced the challenge of adjusting from a suppliers market to a buyers market. Customers have demanded better products at lower costs. Competition from Japan and other Far Eastern countries and from Western Europe have caused many American companies to rebuild their factories, making their manufacturing processes more flexible and efficient with a heightened emphasis on producing quality goods. These changes have required new management approaches, operating controls and financial analysis. Management accounting has had to adapt to this new manufacturing environment.

The research project reported in this volume was sponsored by The IMA Foundation for Applied Research, Inc. (FAR), an affiliate of the Institute of Management Accountants. The project examined the impact that the world-class manufacturing environment has had on the management accounting function and how the management accounting function contributed to the success of world-class manufacturers.

The researchers studied eight organizations that received the Shingo Prize for Excellence in Manufacturing to find answers to these issues. This research report presents the findings. The research centers on the need to develop more actual case situations, so organizations can see what other organizations have done to enhance accounting support of their manufacturing operations.

Our research study findings provide the reader with a variety of approaches used to streamline the management accounting system. The study describes current management accounting practices and the changes these companies have made to eliminate the perceived nonvalue-added procedures. It shows how the management accountant today can be a major contributor to management in the creation of a world-class manufacturing operation.

We hope that this research project will give management accountants additional ideas that they might apply in their organizations to better meet the challenges of the new manufacturing environment.

Acknowledgments

A research project such as this relies heavily on the willingness of plant managers and other busy business people to give a significant amount of their time to complete questionnaires, explain the operations of their businesses, and answer probing questions.

Specifically, appreciation is given for participation in this study to Dana Corporation-Mobile Fluid Products Division; Iomega Corporation; Lifeline Systems, Inc.; AT&T Power Systems; United Electric Controls, Inc.; Glacier Vandervell, Inc.; Wilson Sporting Goods Co.; and Gates Rubber Company. Each of these organizations has received the Shingo Prize for Excellence in Manufacturing. The Shingo Prize is administered by the Business Relations Office in the College of Business at Utah State University. Appreciation is given to Dr. Ross E. Robson, executive director of the Shingo Prize for Excellence in Manufacturing, for his encouragement and assistance in providing background information on the participating organizations. The research team would also like to thank Gayle Brackner for her valuable assistance in editing this manuscript.

A preliminary study for this project was funded by the Research Office of Utah State University. Through that study, the groundwork was laid for a proposal to the Institute of Management Accountants, whose Committee on Research (the predecessor to FAR) made this study possible by providing a research grant to fund the project.

About the Authors

Richard L. Jenson

Richard L. Jenson is an associate professor in the School of Accountancy at Utah State University. He received his Ph.D. from the University of Utah. He is also a Certified Public Accountant licensed by the state of Utah. His business experience included six years in public accounting and one year in health-care accounting.

At present, Dr. Jenson serves as a member of the Shingo Prize Board of Examiners. He teaches both graduate and undergraduate classes in the area of accounting systems. His research interests include accounting systems support in manufacturing environments, management of end-user computing, and software effort estimation. His research articles have appeared in *Journal of Systems and Software, Corporate Controller, Accountant's Journal, Journal of Accounting and Computers, Managerial Auditing Journal,* and *Information and Management.*

James W. Brackner, CMA

James W. Brackner is a professor, associate director of the School of Accountancy, and director of the Master of Accounting program at Utah State University. He received his Ph.D. from the University of Alabama and his M.S. and B.S. degrees in accounting from Brigham Young University. Dr. Brackner is a Certified Management Accountant and a Certified Public Accountant licensed by the state of Utah. His experience in business has included three years with a Big Six CPA firm and eight years as the chief financial officer of three corporations.

He has served the Institute of Management Accountants as a national director and on four national committees: research, academic relations, ethics, and education. At present he is serving on the ICMA Board of Regents.

Dr. Brackner teaches both graduate and undergraduate classes in the area of managerial accounting. His research interests include business ethics and managerial accounting. Among the journals in which his research has appeared are *The Accounting Review, Contract Management, Management Accounting, Managerial Auditing Journal, Research in Third World Accounting,* and *The Journal of Business Forecasting: Methods and Systems.*

Clifford R. Skousen, CMA

Clifford R. Skousen is Ernst & Young professor and head of the School of Accountancy at Utah State University. He received his Ph.D. from Golden Gate University, his MBA from Pepperdine University, and his B.S. from Brigham Young University. Prior to becoming an academician, he was employed with KPMG Peat Marwick.

Dr. Skousen has been actively involved in several professional organizations including the Institute of Management Accountants, the American Accounting Association, the Federation of Schools of Accountancy, and the Utah Association of CPAs. He served as the national president of Beta Alpha Psi for 1995-96.

His teaching and research interests include management accounting, international accounting, and governmental accounting. Among the journals in which Dr. Skousen's research articles have appeared are *The Accounting Review, Accounting Organizations and Society, Management Accounting, Municipal Finance Journal, Financial Accountability and Management,* and *Journal of Accounting and Computers.*

Table of Contents

Foreword	iii
Preface	v
Acknowledgments	vii
About the Authors	ix
Executive Summary	xv
Chapter 1. The Shingo Prize Manufacturing Environment	1
The Purpose of This Volume	2
The Shingo Prize for Excellence in Manufacturing	3
Developments in World-Class Manufacturing	6
Lean Manufacturing and Management Accounting	9
References	9
Chapter 2. Management Accounting at United Electric Controls, Inc.	11
Introduction	11
Employee Participation and the Concept of Valued Ideas	11
Changes in Manufacturing—Accounting Impacts	12
Production Floor Perspectives on Management Accounting	19
Implications for the Accounting Function	23
Conclusion	25
References	25
Chapter 3. Dana Corporation–Mobile Fluid Products Division	27
Introduction	27
Excellence in Manufacturing: The Dana-Gresen Operating Environment	27
The Changing Information-Reporting Landscape	29
Management Accounting: Doing More with Less	31
Activity-Based Management	34
Accounting Innovation and Improved Operations	35
Accounting Measures of Quality and Productivity	37
Implications of the Dana-Gresen Experience	37
Conclusion	39
References	39

Chapter 4. Proactive Management Accounting at Iomega Corporation — 41

    Introduction — 41
    Proactive Management Accounting Support — 41
    Management Accounting Involvement
        in Modern Production Approaches and Technologies — 42
    MA Support of Other Functional Departments — 44
    Outside Views of Management Accounting — 47
    Future Directions for Management Accounting at Iomega — 49
    Implications for Management Accounting — 51
    Conclusion — 52
    References — 53

Chapter 5. Wilson Sporting Goods Company — 55

    Introduction — 55
    Management Support
        of Total Quality Management Concepts — 57
    Accounting Support of Total Quality Management Concepts — 61
    Implications for the Accounting Function — 66
    Conclusion — 68
    References — 68

Chapter 6. Gates Rubber Company — 69

    Introduction — 69
    Management Support
        of Total Quality Management Concepts — 71
    Accounting Support of Total Quality Management Concepts — 74
    Impressions of Accounting Department Contributions
        to TQM — 76
    Implications for the Accounting Function — 80
    Conclusion — 81
    References — 81
    Chapter 6 Appendix — 82

Chapter 7. Management Accounting Challenges at Glacier Vandervell, Inc. — 87

    Introduction — 87
    The Glacier Vandervell Production Environment — 87
    The Impact of Cellular Manufacturing — 89
    Management Accounting Challenges at Glacier Vandervell — 90
    Implications for Management Accounting — 94
    Conclusion — 95
    References — 96

Chapter 8. The CFO Organization at AT&T Power Systems — 97
Introduction — 97
Organizational Change Within Power Systems — 98
The Power Systems Manufacturing Environment — 98
The Changing Financial Culture — 100
The Power Systems CFO Organization — 102
Implications for Management Accounting — 108
Conclusion — 110
References — 110

Chapter 9. Lifeline Systems, Inc. — 111
Introduction — 111
System Integration—System Reliance — 112
Q^{10} from an Accounting Perspective — 116
Innovative Accounting Support at Lifeline — 117
Future Challenges and Opportunities for Accounting — 122
The Lifeline Experience—Discussion and Implications — 125
Conclusion — 127
References — 127

Chapter 10. The Shingo Management Accounting Profile — 129
The Integration of Business and Manufacturing Cultures — 129
The Recognition of Lean Manaufacturing and
 Its Effects on Management Accounting Measurements — 129
Continuous Accounting Improvement — 131
The Elimination of Accounting Waste — 131
Toward a Proactive Management Accounting Culture — 133

Appendix 1. Research Methodology
The Methodology — 137
References — 138

Appendix 2. Advance Questionnaire and Site-Visit Discussion Guide — 139
The Questionnaire — 140

Executive Summary

The management accounting profession has been severely criticized in recent years for being slow to respond to significant changes in manufacturing technology and new management philosophies. These critics suggest that manufacturing competitiveness has been hampered by the failure of the management accounting function to support production operations adequately with timely and relevant information. Nevertheless, some firms have succeeded in enhancing their competitive position in world markets by adopting modern manufacturing practices and new management philosophies.

The eight Shingo Prize recipients examined in this study appear to have effectively integrated continuous improvement methodologies throughout the organization. As a result, the accounting functions within these companies have been successful at eliminating nonvalue-added activities, continuously improving accounting processes, developing proactive information support strategies, and challenging procedural accounting artifacts.

Just as individual production cells strive for continuous improvement, reduced setup times, and elimination of nonvalue-added activities, the accounting functions within the Shingo manufacturers have been able to accomplish corresponding objectives by eliminating accounting wastes such as unnecessary transaction processing, excessive paper handling, unnecessary reports, outdated controls and procedures, and excessive historical analysis. Virtually all accounting functions were serving their organization with fewer resources than before.

Study results suggest that the empowerment of the manufacturing cells has important implications for the accounting function in that the manufacturing cells are now assuming responsibility for collecting and analyzing data pertaining to the control of manufacturing operations. Nevertheless, management accounting retains the responsibility for correlating operational measures with financial impact.

Additional results from this field study suggest that reductions in manufacturing cycle times, changes to cellular manufacturing, and the implementation of just-in-time systems have reduced the need for much of the detailed transaction processing associated with tracking work-in-process inventories. As a result, accountants must reevaluate the benefits of traditional costing measurements in light of modern manufacturing processes. Furthermore, accountants must be careful that the tracking of internal transactions and the measurement of resource utilization are not creating perverse incentives or perpetuating barriers to continuous improvement within the organization.

Finally, the study findings suggest that accountants must develop methods to measure the prospective financial impact of employee actions. It is no longer sufficient for accountants to present the financial results of operations in retrospect. In addition, accountants must use modern computer technology properly and dismantle the manual and paper-intensive systems they are supposed to replace as well as reevaluate procedural artifacts that hinder business productivity.

1

The Shingo Prize Manufacturing Environment

Severe criticism of the accounting profession has raised serious doubts about its long-term viability. Although the management accounting function historically has played an important role in providing operating managers with the information needed to make decisions, the profession appears to be struggling with major changes in the industrial, economic, and technological landscapes:

➤ Competitive pressures in an increasingly global market have made it imperative for businesses to make continual improvements in both product quality and production efficiency.

➤ Technological advances and the emergence of new management paradigms have exerted a significant influence on the competitive structure of virtually all industries.

➤ Robotics and other computerized production technologies have eliminated the labor intensiveness of many production processes.

➤ Manufacturing philosophies such as just-in-time (JIT), total quality commitment, and zero waste have had a significant impact on manufacturing methodologies.

Yet, according to some academicians and practitioners, management accountants have not provided decision-making information to managers that is relevant in light of new manufacturing and production paradigms. Johnson and Kaplan (1987) claim that "... management accounting information is produced too late, too aggregated, and too distorted to be relevant for managers' planning and control decisions...." (p. 22) For example, Cooper and Kaplan (1988) have demonstrated how outdated costing approaches can lead to less-than-optimal decisions.

Other researchers propose various strategies for making management accounting more relevant. Boer (1991) suggests that accounting should undergo the same cost/benefit scrutiny as other functional areas.

Such scrutiny should eliminate accounting activities that either promote dysfunctional behavior within the organization or fail to lead to higher-quality products or more efficient production processes. McNair and Carr (1991) emphasize that management accounting should go beyond placing a value on inventory for financial reporting purposes. They suggest that the development of a system to measure the cost of quality is an example of an accounting activity with potential for adding value to the firm.

Convey (1991) and Turney (1992) describe several approaches for analyzing the relevance and value-added nature of accounting activities. Opportunities also appear to exist for management accountants to improve decision support by providing managers with information across multiple dimensions such as products, distribution channels, and customers (Cooper & Kaplan 1991, Rolfe 1992). Similarly, supporting higher-level decision making such as strategic planning offers a significant opportunity for accountants that has yet to be effectively exploited (Bromwich 1990).

The Purpose of This Volume

The increasing complexity and uncertainty confronting modern business operating environments has fueled the demand for increasingly sophisticated information support. While the management accounting profession scrambles to regain relevance in the modern manufacturing environment, it is clear that some innovative companies have already achieved levels of excellence in their manufacturing methodologies. For example, prestigious awards such as the Malcolm Baldrige National Quality Award and the Shingo Prize for Excellence in American Manufacturing have been bestowed upon American manufacturers that have achieved world-class status in competitiveness. Nevertheless, the role management accounting has played in these successful organizations is not clearly understood.

To more fully understand the contributions made by management accounting to manufacturing excellence, the researchers conducted a study of eight Shingo Prize winners (see Exhibit 1-1) to answer the following questions:

➢ What impact has the world-class manufacturing environment had on the management accounting function?
➢ How has the management accounting function contributed to the success of these world-class manufacturers?

This volume documents the results of site visits to eight Shingo Prize recipients that agreed to participate in this study. The remainder of this chapter describes the Shingo Prize for Excellence in Manufacturing and the manufacturing environment forming the basis of this study.

The Shingo Prize Manufacturing Environment 3

Exhibit 1-1. Participating Shingo Prize Winners

> - AT&T Microelectronics Power Systems, Mesquite, Texas (1992)
> - Dana Mobile Fluid Products Division, Minneapolis, Minnesota (1991)
> - Gates Rubber Company, Siloam Springs, Arkansas (1993)
> - Glacier Vandervell, Inc., Atlantic, Iowa (1991)
> - Iomega Corporation, Roy, Utah (1992)
> - Lifeline Systems, Inc., Cambridge, Massachusetts (1991)
> - United Electric Controls Company, Watertown, Massachusetts (1990)
> - Wilson Sporting Goods Company, Humboldt, Tennessee (1993)

The Shingo Prize for Excellence in Manufacturing

The Shingo Prize for Excellence in Manufacturing was established in 1988 to recognize North American companies that have demonstrated excellence in productivity and process improvement, quality enhancement, and customer satisfaction. The overriding philosophy of the Shingo Prize is that world-class manufacturing status is achieved by:

- Focusing on core manufacturing processes;
- Implementing lean, flexible production systems;
- Eliminating waste;
- Achieving zero defects.

At the same time, the award fosters continuous product improvement and continuous cost reduction (Robson 1991).

■ Shigeo Shingo

The Shingo Prize is named for the late Japanese industrial engineer, international consultant, and author, Dr. Shigeo Shingo. Shingo is credited with playing a key role (along with Taiichi Ohno) in the development of the Toyota JIT production system. In addition to JIT, he is renowned for manufacturing process improvement methodologies such as single-minute exchange of die (SMED) and *poka yoke* (mistake proofing) (Shingo 1992). Shingo aggressively targeted wasteful manufacturing practices and classified them as the seven basic categories of waste: overproduction, waiting for machines, transportation time, process time, excess inventory, excess motion, and defects (Shingo Prize Council 1993).

■ The Shingo Prize Model of Manufacturing

The Shingo Prize Achievement Criteria are divided into four major categories, based on the Shingo Prize Model of Manufacturing (Exhibit 1-2). The premise of the model is that the total quality and productivity management culture and infrastructure (category I) leads to the implementation of world-class manufacturing strategies, processes, and systems (category II). In turn, these strategies, processes, and systems should result in measured improvements in quality and productivity (category III). Finally, the ultimate measure of manufacturing success is viewed in this model as customer satisfaction (category IV).

Challengers for the prize must document their accomplishments within each of these categories in an achievement report submitted to the Shingo Prize Board of Examiners. The achievement reports are scored according to procedures outlined in the Shingo Prize Application Guidelines. Finalists emerging from this evaluation process are further evaluated during a site visit conducted by a team of examiners (Shingo Prize Council 1993).

Exhibit 1-2. The Shingo Prize Model of Manufacturing

I. Total Quality and Productivity Management Culture	II. Manufacturing Processes and Systems	III. Measured Quality and Productivity
• Leading • Empowering • Partnering	• Manufacturing vision/strategy • Mfg. process integration • Quality and productivity methods • Manufacturing and business integration	• Quality enhancement • Productivity improvement

IV. Measured Customer Satisfaction

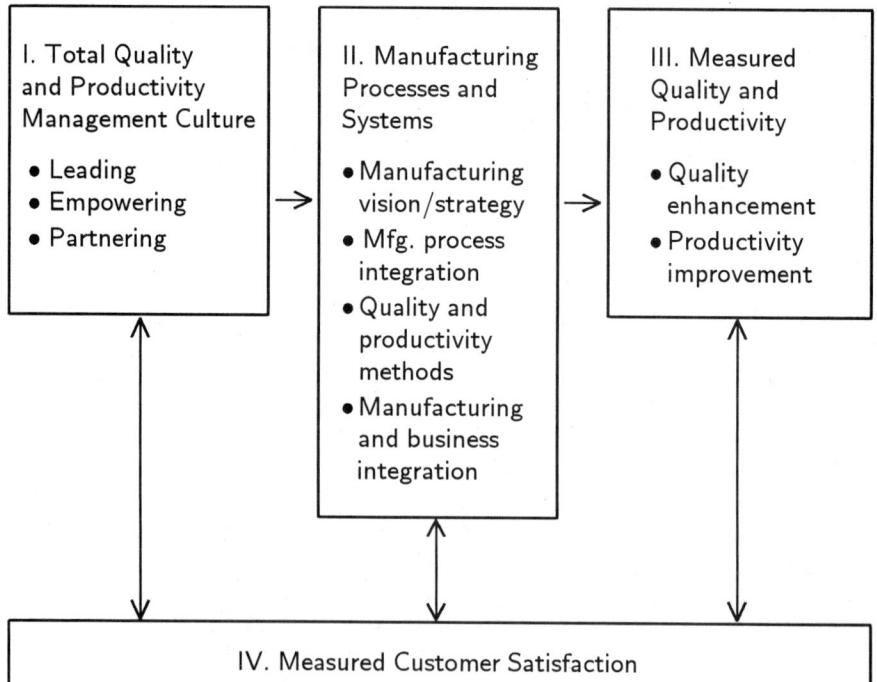

■ Key Evaluation Factors

Several of the key evaluation factors pertaining to each achievement category are discussed briefly below:

Total quality and productivity management culture and infrastructure. This category includes the concepts of leading, empowering, and partnering.

Leading refers to methods by which the company communicates its statements of mission, strategy, goals, and policies to its employees. Leading includes management involvement and leadership in the areas of quality enhancement, productivity improvement, and customer satisfaction. Shingo Prize challengers also should show evidence that the company philosophy encourages and recognizes innovations and improvements.

Empowering includes the education of employees in lean manufacturing methodologies and philosophies. In addition, formal teams of employees are engaged to identify and solve problems and improve processes. Employee suggestions are encouraged and rewarded. Overall employee satisfaction also becomes a key measure within this achievement category.

Partnering refers to the actions taken by the organization to strengthen partner relationships with relevant stakeholders. It may include the improved interface with suppliers to obtain better materials and delivery performance and with customers to improve quality, productivity, and customer satisfaction. In addition, partnering may include benchmarking with other organizations to identify best practices within the industry.

Manufacturing strategy, processes, and system integration. The Shingo Prize criteria focus heavily on the core manufacturing processes of the candidate firm. A manufacturing vision should be evident and linked to the selection of specific methods, systems, and processes. The candidate firms must document the realignment of manufacturing practices that lead to measurable improvements. Examiners look for the successful implementation of such methods as JIT, cellular process arrangement, continuous flow manufacturing, and systematic waste elimination programs.

The challenger's achievement report also must document specific manufacturing processes and tools aimed at achieving the objectives of lean manufacturing. Examples of such tools are source inspection and mistake proofing, visual controls, and statistical process control. It is particularly important for a candidate firm to demonstrate that its lean manufacturing philosophies and methods are integrated throughout the organization, including nonmanufacturing functions such as customer service, finance, and engineering.

Measured quality and productivity. Challengers for the prize must document improvements in productivity and quality. Examples of productivity might include (but not be limited to) labor productivity, materials yield, inventory turnover, and cycle and lead-time reductions. Appropriate quality measures might include the cost of quality, measures of process variation, downtime, and warranty costs.

Measured customer satisfaction. Documented improvements in customer satisfaction might include such measures as customer reject rates, shipment errors, on-time delivery, customer surveys, and customer awards.

Developments in World-Class Manufacturing

As suggested by the award criteria, several concepts, described below, have been key to the success of many of the Shingo Prize recipients. Becoming familiar with them will help readers to understand the individual case studies presented in later chapters.

Total quality management (TQM). Successful companies have come to realize that providing high-quality products improves customer satisfaction (and therefore market share) and saves the company money lost through warranty costs, repairs, and rework. Approaches to quality control have moved away from end-of-process inspection to quality that is designed and built into the product and processes. An important part of TQM is the philosophy of continuous improvement (Japanese term: *kaizen*) whereby company employees have assumed more responsibility for identifying ways to improve both the products and the production processes.

Customer focus. Japanese companies have focused on developing, designing, building, and servicing products that are most economical, useful, and satisfactory to the customer.

Empowerment. Excellent companies have learned that production cells need to be given considerable autonomy and responsibility for their own operations. The cell workers assume the responsibility for configuring their processes, setting their work assignments, and measuring and reporting their own quality and productivity. The workers at the cell level, it is believed, know their operations the best and therefore are the most qualified to suggest methods for improving their processes.

Cellular manufacturing. With the cellular manufacturing approach, individual manufacturing cells are configured to produce a family of products. Each cell contains the machinery necessary just for that group of products. Contrast this configuration with the traditional approach in which different machining departments are set up and a product is routed through each functional department. The cellular approach allows management to focus more on product-line productivity than on machine efficiencies.

Nonstock production. Shigeo Shingo believed that companies should produce sufficient products to fill existing orders and no more. He believed the practice of filling warehouses with inventory that had no immediate buyer was wasteful, for several reasons:

➤ Inventory ties up working capital;
➤ Maintaining a warehouse to store the surplus goods is expensive;
➤ The movement of the goods to and from the warehouse is wasted effort;
➤ Goods may become obsolete as they sit waiting for a buyer.

Pull systems. The concept of pull systems, also espoused by Shingo, is closely related to the concept of nonstock production. It suggests that market forces should "pull" the products out of the factories. In other words, customers order the merchandise and we manufacture to meet that order. The opposite approach, the "push" system, manufactures the product and then pushes it out into the market in hopes of finding a buyer for it.

Cycle time. The key to nonstock production is the ability to respond quickly to customer orders. Obviously, a manufacturer that does not maintain large inventories must be able to produce a complete customer order within a few hours or days. Cycle time refers to the time a product requires to navigate the entire production process, from materials introduction to packing and delivery.

Single-minute exchange of die (SMED). SMED is another Shingo concept concerned with reducing machine setup time on the production line. A *die* is a device that forms, stamps, or cuts metal to set specifications. A machine may be fitted with different sizes of interchangeable dies that allow the machine to be used on different products. The idea with SMED is to design the dies so that the machine can be changed over in a matter of minutes. When machines require several hours for changeover there is a temptation to "stamp out" extra parts to maintain the efficiency levels of the machine. SMED gives the production line more flexibility in moving from one part or product to another.

Just-in-time (JIT). Toyota was the earliest and arguably the most successful champion of the JIT manufacturing system. Former Toyota chairman, Taiichi Ohno, and production engineer, Shigeo Shingo, were the key architects of the Toyota production system. With JIT, parts and materials reach the production cell as they are needed in the process. With the exception of small buffer stocks, inventories are not maintained. JIT requires close coordination between manufacturer and supplier to synchronize materials shipments with production activities.

Kanban. Kanban is the Japanese word for a sign or card that authorizes the movement of goods from one manufacturing cell to another. One way to think of a kanban is as a stock replenishment signal that establishes a dynamic customer/supplier relationship. It tends to be a visually oriented system that establishes maximum in-process inventory levels, limits daily production quotas, or indicates the reorder point for materials. The kanban might be a stack of trays located between manufacturing cells where work-in-process (WIP) is held temporarily until moved to the next process. The trays typically will be designed to hold a maximum number of units. When the out tray is filled by an upstream cell, production in that process stops until the tray is "relieved" by a downstream cell. This physical mechanism prevents a production cell from overproducing or producing to stock. From an inventory reorder perspective, the kanban serves as a flag to reorder a specific quantity of raw materials or parts. For example, when a part level drops to a preestablished level, the kanban card is used to contact the vendor to replenish the stock.

Poka yoke. Poka yoke is a Japanese term for "mistake proofing." A poka-yoke device prevents mistakes from being made during the production process. An example is a drilling template that prevents the drill press operator from mounting the product backwards on the machine and then drilling the holes in the wrong place, thus causing scrap. Shigeo Shingo has placed considerable emphasis in his writings on mistake proofing.

Lead time. In the context of a customer, lead time refers to the estimated time a customer must allow for the delivery of ordered merchandise. Many of the Shingo Prize winners have reduced their customer delivery lead times from several months to three to four weeks. Clearly, the shorter the lead time, the more flexible the manufacturing process can be.

Value-added activity. An activity performed within the organization is value-added if it adds value to the products or services of the company. To determine if an activity is value-added or not, the following question can be asked: Would our customer be willing to pay extra for the activity in question? If the answer is no, the activity is not value-added.

Backflush. In many modern organizations, production cycle times have been reduced to such a point that it no longer serves any purpose to maintain detailed transaction records on the movement of WIP inventory through the production system. As a practical matter, the product would be finished and on a delivery truck before the work-in-process inventory reports reflected its movement or present status. Therefore, the extra effort to record and process these additional transactions is no longer justified.

The backflush approach simply relieves (in the accounting sense) materials inventory of the items that should have been consumed during the production run for a product or batch of products. The backflush is triggered at the time the product is packaged and ready for shipment. As a result, detailed transactions are not recorded every time a piece of raw material is introduced into the manufacturing process or moves from process to process.

Lean Manufacturing and Management Accounting

Clearly, the spread of lean manufacturing principles has begun to affect the practice of management accounting significantly. As will be shown in the chapters that follow, the management accounting function within the Shingo culture has been forced to integrate many of the same concepts as its manufacturing counterparts. The authors hope that the experiences of these companies provide positive examples of how management accounting can make this transition.

References

Boer, G. B. 1991. Making accounting a value-added activity. *Management Accounting*, August, 73(2), pp. 36-41.

Bromwich, M. 1990. The case for strategic management accounting: the role of accounting information for strategy in competitive markets. *Accounting, Organizations, and Society*, 15(1/2), pp. 27-46.

Convey, S. 1991. Eliminating unproductive activities and processes. *CMA Magazine*, November, pp. 20-24.

Cooper, R., & Kaplan, R.S. 1988. Measure costs right: make the right decisions. *Harvard Business Review*, 66, pp. 96-103.

Cooper, R., & Kaplan, R.S. 1991. Profit priorities from activity-based costing. *Harvard Business Review*, 169, pp. 130-135.

Cooper, R., & Kaplan, R. S. 1992. Activity-based systems: measuring the costs of resource usage. *Accounting Horizons*, 6(3), pp. 1-13.

Johnson, H.T., & Kaplan, R.S. 1987. The rise and fall of management accounting. *Management Accounting*, January, 68(7), pp. 22-30.

King, A. M. 1991. The current status of activity-based costing: an interview with Robin Cooper and Robert S. Kaplan. *Management Accounting*, September, 73(3), pp. 22-26.

McNair, C. J., & Carr, L. 1991. Toward value-added management accounting. *CMA Magazine*, April, 65(3), pp. 26-28.

Robson, R. E. 1991. The Shingo Prize: Excellence in manufacturing. *Target*, 7(4), pp. 28-30.

Rolfe, A. J. 1992. Profitability reporting techniques bridge information gap. *The Journal of Business Strategy*, 13, pp. 32-36.

Shingo, S. 1992. *The Shingo production management system: Improving process functions* (A.P. Dillon, trans.). Cambridge, Massachusetts: Productivity Press, Inc. (original work published 1990).

Shingo Prize Council. 1993. *Shingo Prize for Excellence in Manufacturing: 1993-1994 application guidelines.*

Turney, Peter B.B. 1992. Activity-based management. *Management Accounting*, January, 73(7), pp. 20-25.

2
Manufacturing Excellence Through Valued Ideas

Management Accounting at United Electric Controls, Inc.

Introduction

Founded in 1931, United Electric Controls, Inc. (UE), located in Watertown, Massachusetts, manufactures electronic and electromechanical temperature and pressure controls and sensors. In 1985, UE established a manufacturing education function to introduce a lean manufacturing culture. The company-wide improvement process was initiated in 1986 to facilitate continuous improvement activities throughout the plant. The plant has documented numerous achievements resulting from broad-based continuous improvement methodologies. Among them are:

- 50% inventory reduction in three years;
- WIP reduction from $1.2 million to $300,000;
- On-time deliveries increase from 60% to 95%;
- Lead time reduction from 10 weeks to two weeks; 60% shipped within three days;
- Part standardization improvement of 33%;
- 10,000% increase in employee participation;
- 90% voluntary participation.

As a result of these and many other achievements, UE was awarded the 1990 Shingo Prize for Excellence in Manufacturing.

Employee Participation and the Concept of Valued Ideas

Employee participation has been a key factor in the continued success of UE. UE employees are encouraged to participate on cross-functional teams formed to tackle specific problems within the plant. Intellectual contributions from employees also are strongly encouraged. One of the most important vehicles for employee participation is known at UE as the *valued idea*. Employees are encouraged to submit ideas for process improvements and waste elimination. Employees are recognized for submitting valued ideas and receive gifts and prizes for those ideas that actually are implemented.

Indeed, many valued ideas are very simple. In one case, a workcell employee suggested that tooling mounted on a lazy Susan would save both space and wasted motion within the work cell. Another valued idea, a poka-yoke device, was simply a cardboard template placed over parts bins within the cell to prevent the wrong components from being inserted into the product. UE encourages employees to continually find areas for small improvements rather than to wait for a breakthrough solution.

Employees have additional incentives to contribute valued ideas. According to UE Vice President of Finance Brian Hallahan, if an employee comes up with an idea that results in time savings, it does not necessarily mean that the persons affected simply will be given other tasks to fill the free time. Time savings realized through the implementation of an employee's valued idea can be used by that employee for personal improvement, study, or other participation in quality programs throughout the plant (Hallahan 1993).

Changes in Manufacturing—Accounting Impacts

Vice President of Operations Bruce Hamilton observes that accounting has been affected by lean manufacturing methods in the same fashion as other manufacturing and service departments—there are fewer of them. They are doing more with less by identifying and eliminating wasteful practices. He notes that the accounting function has participated in the same continuous improvement activities as the rest of the company (Hamilton 1993).

Cost Accounting Manager Alan Waugh notes that accounting has had to react to manufacturing changes. Management has the responsibility to get the orders in, get the product built, and get the units out the door. Accounting has to accommodate that process without restricting manufacturing operations (Waugh 1993).

■ Product Cost Implications of JIT

The philosophy of JIT means that less inventory is maintained, and there is less need for a stockroom, for stockroom people, for people who kit[1] the job, and for people in shipping. The people who used to move the materials back and forth are no longer needed. As a result, the computation of product cost has been affected because some departmental activities have been changed from overhead activities to direct-labor activities. The activity of picking the stock is now the worker's responsibility. Also, packing the product, formerly an overhead activity, is now considered a direct-labor cost within the production cell. Without adjustment for changing manufacturing practices, distortions in costs and cost ratios can result (Hallahan 1993).

UE used to have a $250,000 picking machine that occupied significant floor space. Jobs were kitted and taken out to the floor for assembly. With cellular manufacturing, the parts are kept in the areas where they are used. Not only is the effort of picking, kitting, and bagging saved, but the costs and floor space associated with the picking machine are eliminated (Regal 1993).

The continuous improvement culture at UE has freed up manufacturing time that can be used for employee development and further improvements in the production process. Furthermore, cell workers are not asked to separate time spent on different products, time spent on quality team meetings, time spent on personal study, or other nonmanufacturing time. All time is considered direct. Hallahan emphasizes that you can analyze labor cost to the nth degree without significant savings because it represents only 10% of the selling price. As a result, UE prefers to focus on overhead costs rather than direct labor, because the overhead costs are twice the labor cost.

Although activity-based costing (ABC) has not been applied at UE, many of the concepts of ABC have been accounted for in changing work patterns and manufacturing cell configurations. For example, the movement of the product back and forth between stock and the manufacturing cell is nonvalue-added activity. Locating stock in the work cell along with the packing function eliminates excess product movement. Thus, the essence of ABC is implemented without applying it as such.

Waugh suggests that management must decide the extent to which it will commit to expensive financial or activity-based costing systems. Furthermore, he asks, after spending significant resources on software, hardware, additional personnel, and outside consulting, will management use these systems?

---

[1] Kitting refers to the preassembly withdrawal (from inventory) of materials/components needed to assemble a complete product. The kits then are transported to the assembly point. The Shingo manufacturing culture has come to view this packing and transporting operation as wasted effort because the storage and selection of assembly parts now takes place within the manufacturing cell.

While UE never had a "true" cost accounting system in place, the company did require workers to fill out labor tickets up until 1987. At that time, the manufacturing vice president decided he wanted the workers to spend their time in a more productive manner. Rather than filling out labor tickets, the attention of the workers would be refocused on getting the product out the door. The company changed hourly workers to salaried workers, and labor reports, such as labor efficiency, were no longer produced (Waugh 1993).

■ Simplified Account Structures

Formerly, UE had 97 departments and five divisions. Management noticed that many of these departments had only one or two employees. A quality team was assembled to look at reducing the number of departments and the account numbers driven by them. For each department, 10 accounts had to be maintained, so a reduction of 10 departments would save 100 account numbers. Formerly the company maintained 10 to 12 direct-labor departments; now only five direct-labor departments are tracked. Previously, many pages of overhead departments were broken down between electronics and mechanical; now the distinction is not considered significant.

According to Waugh:

> We have cut down on the number of general ledger accounts. We have cut down the number of departments we used to have. With the number of accounts we used to have, you would have thought we were General Motors. We had eighty or ninety departments, one-man bands, if you will. We don't need that kind of reporting. We are not General Motors.

■ Simplified Transaction Processing

Hallahan describes the need to simplify work-in-process accounting:

> You take a product from the raw materials stage, you build it in a day, and then you put a transaction through at the end of the day to pull it right through work-in-process and into finished goods. Because the manufacturing process happens so fast, you don't bother following the transactions with paper. Why move the product five times on paper when the product is gone before the paper is processed?

Electronics Operations Manager John Paul Williams relates that formerly UE floor workers completed cost cards to record the component materials and parts that went into each job. Similarly, employees used to complete time sheets to show the amount of labor that went into each job. He believes the cost of data-collection efforts exceeded the benefits realized (Williams 1993).

Management Accounting at United Electric Controls, Inc.

The UE accounting department used to spend significant effort tracking vacation expense over the fiscal period. They have since determined that the level did not fluctuate enough to warrant a monthly accounting adjustment. Hallahan says, "If it's an estimate, treat it as an estimate. Let's be relevant to the left of the decimal point."

■ Educating the Factory

When it comes to specific product-costing information, the cost accounting function at UE makes sure the product information is correct so it can be used directly by other departments within UE. Because UE operates in an original equipment manufacturer (OEM) environment, it is constantly receiving requests for product cost and pricing data. Making this database available outside the accounting department (for example, to sales and customer service), means that the cost accountant no longer has to be involved each time to look up the information (Hallahan 1993).

Hallahan also notes that accounting at UE has educated the engineers: now they know that it is not always the best decision to factor in a new screw at a half-cent savings over an existing one, because now you have a new part to track as well as a new vendor. Another reason for staying with an existing screw is the possibility of obtaining additional volume discounts that may offset the alleged savings associated with the new screw.

In addition, ripple effects occur throughout the organization. For example, if the variety of inventory parts is reduced, then the number of vendors is reduced, there are fewer checks to write, a smaller inventory space is required, and there are fewer phone calls to expedite parts orders.

Waugh notes that manufacturing has conducted variety effectiveness analysis to reduce the number of parts in the system. New parts cause the proliferation of drawings (to engineer the new part), inventory, part numbers, and so on. The number of items in the master file is actually an effectiveness measure as the company attempts to limit the number of active inventory items. Waugh works closely with the materials control manager and drafting to help push the number of parts down and remove inactive or obsolete parts from the master file. In addition, drawings of inactive parts are archived and removed from the drawings file so that an engineer searches a comparatively small set of active drawings.

Accounting has analyzed freight expense and has assisted UE in educating individuals and departments about the financial impact of using express mail unnecessarily. Accounting has informed the company about alternatives to express mail (such as second-day air) and the need to plan shipments to avoid overnight delivery expense when possible. In addition, accounting helped negotiate arrangements with some carriers to make shipments more economical (Wallack 1993).

The cost of carrying slow-paying customers has been recognized and measured by the accounting staff at UE. This measure, known as the "cost of payment past 30 days," is computed as the customer sales volume multiplied by the periodic interest rate for the time period the customer is overdue. This measure is included in the reports to the sales staff (Wallack 1993).

■ Eliminating Nonvalue-Added Activities

The Shingo culture fostered at UE encourages a continual reevaluation of all processes. According to Waugh (1993):

> The Shingo manufacturing strategies employed within UE have forced accounting to examine each of our functions and ask: What are we really doing? Is it necessary? Are we gathering information that will be used for record retention? Or are we gathering information that can be used as the basis for decision making? If we are producing reports that are just being filed in a drawer, maybe we are just wasting our time.

Hallahan views the issuance of hundreds of travel expense checks as a waste of effort. As a result, UE has greatly simplified the expense accounting and reporting process for employees who travel. Traveling employees are issued company credit cards to be used for most expenses and a small cash allowance to cover incidental items typically paid for with cash. In addition, flights are booked through one agency and billed directly to UE. In addition to cost savings, employees under this arrangement find it easier because they are not carrying large balances on their personal credit cards for pending travel reimbursement. Also, employees are largely freed from extensive record keeping.

Credit and Collections Manager Robert Wallack (1993) relates that it used to be difficult to motivate departments within UE to resolve credit memorandums involving relatively small dollar amounts. To expedite the processing of these credits, accounting obtained authorization to resolve credits under $100 without obtaining broader approval. To avoid abuse by customers, a report is run showing credits by customer number. This policy change has reduced the time accounting used to spend contacting other departments about unresolved credits.

General Ledger Manager Kelly Tonner (1993) describes how UE has simplified the ordering of office supplies by giving one person the responsibility of ordering supplies on a weekly basis. Previously, anyone could generate a purchase order for supplies. This system generated many separate invoices that then required processing. The new system effectively limits the number of invoices to one each week.

Arrangements have been made with selected suppliers to reduce the number of separate invoices that need processing. One approach has been to do a better job of consolidating orders to a given supplier. Another approach has been to have the vendor consolidate the billing or use a statement billing approach to reduce the number of invoices or statements requiring processing (Tonner 1993).

■ Improving Accounting Processes

The accounting department at UE uses many of the same types of process improvement tools as are employed on the manufacturing floor. One approach is known as CEDAC (Cause and Effect Diagram with the Addition of Cards), a methodology used to analyze problems within a process and identify appropriate solutions. The UE accounting staff has been able to reduce the time to prepare the monthly financial package from 10 working days to two. A CEDAC process was performed to investigate the cause of the excess time. The first question asked in the CEDAC was, "Why are there so many pages?" The users of the monthly package were asked which 10 pages they looked at the most. As a result of this survey, the package was reduced in size from 30 to 13 pages. They found that many of the eliminated pages contained repetitive information presented in different formats. The accounting staff then took steps to continually enhance the format and presentation of the retained pages to keep the package brief and informative (Tonner 1993).

A significant portion of the reduction in financial statement closing time was achieved by cutting off the payroll entries a week earlier. Before, the accounting staff would wait for the most recent payroll report to make journal entries, which alone held up the process for four days. They decided to use the previous week's report for closing cutoff (with consistent application, accuracy is not materially compromised). The close also was expedited by giving priority-run status to reports needed for the closing process. This decision eliminated the need to hold up the closing while waiting for essential reports (Tonner 1993).

Wallack participated in an action team to analyze why credit memorandums were issued. The four most frequent causes of credits were:
- Incorrect discounts,
- Incorrect pricing,
- Incorrect material returns,
- Defective material returns.

Discount errors were reduced by simplifying the discount structure. Pricing errors were reduced by introducing a price quotation system. A customer complaint system was set up to track the details for defects returns.

Wallack notes that accounting also has developed poka yoke devices in the context of the accounting system. For example, there used to be a problem with incorrect sales tax being computed because the sales discount field was right next to the sales tax field. Too often, the discount rate was being entered by mistake into the field for the sales tax rate. The poka yoke device was a programming control that prevented a sales tax rate of greater than 9% from being entered into this field.

Another poka yoke device was developed to suppress invoices with zero balances from being printed and mailed out. Prior to this new control, sales representatives in the field would be sent invoices with zero amounts because they had received a package of sample products.

In another example of poka yoke, the order entry system was programmed to print out an exception listing when an order is taken without entering a customer purchase order number. This list prevents such transactions from being input into the system without an audit trail.

UE has placed the payroll administrator in the personnel department. Prior to this change, inquiries from employees typically would be directed initially to someone in personnel, who would often have to call payroll in accounting. Payroll would reply to personnel, who then would reply to the employee. This middleman communications function was removed when payroll was moved physically into the personnel office. Tonner observes that this maneuver is consistent with what is happening on the shop floor; people are moved to where they can be more effective in the flow of the work.

■ **Increased Accounting Productivity**

The number of full-time equivalent employees (FTE) in accounts payable has been reduced from 3.5 to 1. Formerly, two check runs were required per week to fulfill vendor discount terms. In many cases, a vendor was receiving two checks every week. Tonner observes that the additional check volume resulted in more checks to write, stuff into envelopes, reconcile, file, and so on. Moving to one run per week has reduced the weekly number of checks from 300 to 200 without compromising vendor discounts.

Tonner also notes that the UE accounting staff has successfully absorbed the additional work load of an acquired Connecticut firm, thereby eliminating one accounting position for that entity.

■ **Broadening the Accountant's Horizon**

Despite having no previous manufacturing experience, Tonner was given the opportunity to serve as team leader for an action team responsible for bringing a new product into production. Her team brought together two production employees from the floor, a buyer, an engineer, a manufacturing engineer, and a marketing person. This assignment continued for six months, during which time she performed no accounting functions. In addition to receiving valuable manufacturing background, Tonner brought a questioning attitude back to the accounting department. Tonner suggests that by continually asking why, a lot of "junk" can be eliminated from a job.

Tonner's goal is to have her staff become involved in UE team projects outside the accounting area. Tonner's admonition to her staff is "you work *in* finance, but you work *for* United Electric. . . . Go find out what's going on in this company." She has also brought in sales representatives to give presentations to her staff on the types of products being produced at UE. She has found that this knowledge helps tie operations together and give accounting employees an idea about where UE fits in the marketplace. It also brings to life the products, manufacturing components, customers, and vendors. Rather than viewing customers, vendors, and products as abstract notations on purchase orders and invoices, the accountants gain an increased appreciation of how these various entities relate to the core activities of the organization.

Production Floor Perspectives on Management Accounting

■ Inherent Dangers of Costing Systems

Hamilton is concerned that reports from accounting systems often have a slant that suggests the best supplier is the one that offers the lowest price per piece. Unfortunately, the system does not ask if the company really needs 1,000 parts at this time (to get the price break).

According to Hamilton, UE does not have what he considers good control over its internal costs. However, he adds that Toyota and Honda do not know exactly what their internal costs are either. They are focused on quality, volume, market share, and designing a good product up front. He states, "If you focus on quality and volume, the costs tend to take care of themselves. If you don't have quality and volume, you can have a cost system, but none of the numbers will ever make any sense."

Hamilton agrees with Goldratt's (1984) claim that cost accounting is often "precisely wrong." He notes that:

> . . . Costing systems compute to four decimals and yet they are off by a mile. . . . It all depends. . . . If you buy a product and sell it right away . . . then the cost has meaning. If you buy parts at any cost and you don't sell them, the cost is meaningless. It is very complex trying to decide whether

a product is making a profit . . . or how we should burden this product with overhead. . . . Clearly direct labor has very little to do with allocating overhead.

Hamilton observes that ABC systems are not in place in world-class companies. He believes these systems are just another way to burden the product. "Here are these other people in the organization who aren't building anything. Let's figure out how to allocate their cost to the product. That kind of system is not in place in any of the world-class companies. . . There ought to be a lesson there."

Hamilton relates an experience that occurred several years ago at UE with one of their subcontracted assemblies, parts thought at one time to require too much assembly space to be manufactured in-house. Meanwhile, however, lean manufacturing methodologies had freed up significant capacity within the plant, resulting in some employees needing work. On paper, the argument was that it was cheaper to have this work done outside. Nevertheless, the subcontracted work was brought back inside the plant without adding additional workers, and the full-time subcontracts coordinator's position was eliminated. However, when costs and overhead were reapplied to these assemblies, the sales people complained that the in-house move had ruined the profitability of this product. At that point the finance people became involved and suggested that "everyone reason together." They concluded that UE had saved $250,000 in annual cash outlay, and that this move had indeed favorably affected the bottom line.

■ Costing Barriers to Continuous Improvement

Williams relates that the former manner in which costs were viewed became a barrier to the continuous improvement process. Using old modes of thinking, it would not have been considered efficient to spend time training employees when they could be spending their time building more products.

Williams believes that by looking at costs in a different way, UE was able to generate the necessary ideas to solve some of its problems. For example, he observes that design decisions typically focus on labor and material costs and ignore perhaps 60% of the life-cycle costs of the product.

> Typically, when labor and materials are the only issue on the product, that means that you would be driven to go out and buy a new microprocessor because it might be five cents cheaper. But if you understand the costs of this . . . for example, the software library that I can't use if I buy a new microprocessor, that's going to cost me $400,000 to exploit this cheaper microprocessor. We need a system that understands that.

Management Accounting at United Electric Controls, Inc.

Williams suggests that an engineer might feel that his or her design creativity is being constrained by a system that provides incentives for variety reduction. On the other hand, the engineer needs to realize that the product being designed must make money. Therefore, the system should show the costs that are associated with the designer's creativity.

To this end, UE uses the concepts of total cost versus purchase price in supplier selection. For example, buying overseas may look cheaper if you are looking only at purchase price. However, when considering the total cost of the product, a company also must consider the loss of engineering flexibility associated with an overseas purchase. It might take three months to initiate an engineering change when an overseas supplier is involved, whereas a local supplier could make the change within days. Often, this responsiveness is key to being able to obtain a new order.

Williams observes that the purchase price versus total cost issue is often very volatile within the organization: "If some salespeople are measured on margin, they're going to want purchase price to be the real goal. If someone is trying to run a department to support many different goals, such as responsiveness to engineering as well as good price, then they will look more at total cost."

Williams suggests that cost accounting systems must be responsive to the life-cycle costs of the product. He describes a product design approach used recently on a new product line. In addition to the usual functional specifications, a target selling price was specified. An additional requirement was that 85% of the components of this new product must come from existing parts inventories. Williams explains that using existing components makes startup costs much smaller by:

➢ Greatly reducing initial inventory purchases,
➢ Making inventory demand build on the existing inventory flow,
➢ Lessening the effort to qualify new suppliers.

Williams (1993) believes that a life-cycle costing system sensitive to these costs would be useful in design decisions.

> If you cost a new product knowing that you are keeping the same process or software calls, . . . when you train new salespeople, they already know the existing product. This [new] product has the look and feel of the old products. . . . This reduces training costs. . . . Customers also need less familiarization with the new product.

■ Total Cost Versus Purchase Price

Richard Cranitch (1993), manager of supply development, emphasizes that it is not enough to look only at a supplier's prices; total acquisition cost must be considered. He would like to be able to compare the cost of doing business with a single supplier versus multiple suppliers. He contends that if a company were to buy all its parts for a particular product line from a single supplier, the cost of doing business would be much less because the company would not generate extra paperwork and would have more leverage with the supplier. Paraphrasing Mark Twain, Cranitch emphasizes, however, that "if you put all your eggs in one basket, you had better watch that basket."

UE has reduced its supplier base from approximately 500 to 175. Their approach is to get assistance from the supplier in reducing procurement costs. For example, UE wants its suppliers to reduce paperwork by allowing the release of materials from a letter of intent (Cranitch 1993).

■ **Linking Operational Measures to Financial Results**

Williams relates that during the training phase of the continuous improvement movement, an attempt was made to connect the financial statement measures to "real" measures that would mean something on the factory floor. Williams believes that the financial statement measures are reliable indicators of how the organization is doing. The tried and true measures in operations, such as utilization rate and dollars per employee, were not accurate indicators of what was happening on the shop floor. UE had to search for a link that tied the financial indicators to measures that made sense on the production floor. Williams relates that the prescribed Goldratt indicators (throughput, inventory levels, and operating expenses) were very helpful in developing such measures. The UE goal was to have assemblers on the floor, as well as everyone in the organization, understand these measures, to develop a business-minded shop floor where costs were understood.

Williams related an example of a CEDAC the company has been working on related to Goldratt's throughput. The throughput measure was used to express to assembly workers that throughput needed to be increased from 60 units per week to 490 units per week. Williams explains that initially, operating expenses will increase as a result of the increased throughput. Then, when the desired throughput is reached and the production line is stabilized, the focus will shift to reducing operating expenses. After operating expenses are brought under control, focus shifts to minimizing inventory levels.

This continuous improvement progression is typical of new production lines at UE. Emphasis is placed first on throughput until throughput stability is reached. Once throughput stability is achieved, focus shifts to reducing operating expenses. With mature lines, emphasis is placed on running with very small inventories. This goal is possible because the marketplace is well known, and inventory needs can be predicted more accurately (Williams 1993).

Williams believes that accounting is the appropriate department for the development of linkage measures (linkage of operational and financial measures). However, he cautions that such data collection must be manageable. Otherwise the system will collapse due to clerical burdens placed on workers.

■ The Critical Nature of Performance Measures

Williams observes that the challenge associated with developing effective gainsharing measures is that localized measures tend to promote local optimization at the expense of the organizational goals. At the other extreme, employees may not be motivated by organizational measures that are so broad as to obscure the measurement of individual contribution. According to Williams:

> You have to be very careful about the measures you pick because you can create conflicts accidentally, rather than measures. If the measures are good, people like them because they prove they are doing a good job. The problem is that the old-time measures don't do that. They don't reflect that people are doing a good job. That's why there was so much vehemence against them. . . . I think people like to be measured. People who have a savings account like to look at the number going up. I think it's a natural instinct. The problem is when people don't trust the measures.

■ Identifying and Reducing Transaction Costs

Paperwork has been reduced in the area of materials acquisition by eliminating the purchase requisition. UE has an area where hardware distributors come in and replenish stocks directly. Because hardware is such a low-cost item, UE has gone to expensing it at the time of purchase without bills of material and other formal issuance procedures. Billing occurs on a monthly basis. As a result the overhead costs associated with the requisition, handling, accounts payable management, and issuance of the hardware have been reduced.

Cranitch would like to see accounting assistance in determining the cost of doing business with a given supplier. He also sees additional opportunities for accountants in identifying the cost of carrying material and the cost of not having material available when needed.

Implications for the Accounting Function

1. Organizations must dismantle product-costing mechanisms that present barriers to continuous improvement. One particularly interesting difference between the Shingo method and traditional American manufacturing culture is the way employee idle time is viewed. The traditional American view has been that workers and machines must be kept constantly busy to maintain respective labor and machine efficiencies, even if the result is excess inventory. Japanese manufacturers tend to view periods of employee idle time as necessary and even desirable. Rather than keeping people and machines busy building excess inventory, the Japanese culture exploits these interludes to train employees and continually improve processes.

Contributing to the traditional American efficiency culture, of course, are cost accounting systems and efficiency measures that actually reward employees for building excess inventory rather than encourage the use of nonproduction time to improve people and production systems. Organizations and accountants must consider carefully what types of activities their present systems are rewarding, and if these systems are hindering continuous improvement efforts.

2. *Accountants should constantly consider ways to simplify transaction processing.* Accountants better than any other group should understand the costs associated with high volumes of transaction processing. The processing of accounting transactions does not build products or satisfy customers. Often, however, production employees can be distracted from their manufacturing activities by burdensome paperwork and data collection. Moreover, with shorter manufacturing cycle times, transactions that track product movement often cannot keep up with the product. Accountants always should be questioning the need for data collection and looking for ways to:

➢ Reduce the number of documents to be processed (purchase orders, checks, invoices);
➢ Simplify the chart of account structures;
➢ Simplify the accruals and other estimates associated with statement closing;
➢ Reduce the opportunity for costly errors in processing.

3. *Accountants must educate the employees about the financial consequences of their actions.* The accountant's understanding of financial impacts must be communicated to employees throughout the organization in a format meaningful to them. For example, accountants can show the financial impact of improper use of express mail, the costs of carrying a delinquent customer, the costs of processing various types of transactions, and the costs of maintaining additional vendors and parts. The challenge and opportunity for accountants is to identify the linkages between operational performance and financial impact and to report them in such a man-

ner that the worker on the floor can be better informed and motivated.

4. *The organization must consider the total cost of materials acquisitions rather than simply the supplier purchase price.* The experiences of UE and others would indicate that in a materials purchase decision, the total or life-cycle cost of that decision goes significantly beyond the simple purchase price offered by the supplier. Not included in the purchase price are costs (or cost savings) associated with doing business with one or many vendors, maintaining a part in inventory, compromising engineering flexibility by using an overseas supplier, designing new products using new versus existing parts, training sales staff and customers, and building leverage with suppliers. Once again, accountants have an opportunity to clarify acquisition decisions.

5. *Accounting must resist becoming isolated from the core activities of the enterprise.* At a time when many are questioning the integrity and relevance of accounting outputs, accountants must aggressively demonstrate an understanding of the core operations. This understanding can be obtained only through involvement in production activities and participation in action teams. Clearly, it will be impossible for accountants to serve as educators to the organization without this level of involvement and understanding of the organization's processes.

Conclusion

An important criterion in the selection of Shingo Prize recipients is the degree to which the tenets of lean manufacturing and continuous improvement are integrated throughout the organization. The accounting department at United Electric Controls, Inc. is an example of the successful integration of Shingo philosophies into a service department. Results of this integration within accounting include transaction processing simplification, elimination of nonvalue-added activities, programs to broaden accounting horizons, programs to continually improve accounting processes, and education of the organization as to the financial impact of their operations.

References

Cranitch, R. 1993. Manager, supply development, United Electric Controls, Inc. On-site interview, May 11-12.

Goldratt, E.M., and Cox, J. 1984. *The Goal: Excellence in Manufacturing.* New York: North River Press, Inc.

Hallahan, B. 1993. Vice president, finance, United Electric Controls, Inc. On-site interview, May 11-12.

Hamilton, B. 1993. Vice president, manufacturing, United Electric Controls, Inc. On-site interview, May 11-12.

Regal, J. 1993. Customer service representative, United Electric Controls, Inc. On-site interview, May 11-12.

Tonner, K. 1993. General ledger manager, United Electric Controls, Inc. On-site interview, May 11-12.

Wallack, R. 1993. Credit and collections manager, United Electric Controls, Inc. On-site interview, May 11-12.

Waugh, A. 1993. Cost accounting manager, United Electric Controls, Inc. On-site interview, May 11-12.

Williams, J. 1993. Electronics operations manager, United Electric Controls, Inc. On-site interview, May 11-12.

3

Management Accounting and Excellence in Manufacturing

Dana Corporation–Mobile Fluid Products Division

Introduction

The Minneapolis plant of Dana Corporation-Mobile Fluid Products Division was founded in 1945 under the name of Gresen Manufacturing. A manufacturer of hydraulic control valves for heavy off-highway equipment, Gresen eventually was acquired by Dana Corporation, in 1981. In 1987, Dana-Gresen embarked on its Excellence in Manufacturing (EIM) program. EIM is a wide-ranging program involving various methods of continuous improvement. Employees have been extensively trained in the EIM philosophy and are involved heavily in its implementation and operation. The success of EIM at Dana-Gresen is evidenced by their receiving the Shingo Prize for Excellence in Manufacturing in 1991.

Excellence in Manufacturing: The Dana-Gresen Operating Environment

Dana-Gresen appears to have benefited significantly from the EIM program first introduced in 1987. EIM principles implemented included cellular manufacturing, employee empowerment, waste elimination, inventory reduction, customer lead-time reduction, increased product quality, and reduced manufacturing setup times.

■ Employee Empowerment — Employee Trust

Each manufacturing cell is allowed to configure its own processes to meet the needs of its internal and external customers. In addition, employees participate as members of interdepartmental EIM teams charged with improving various operations within the plant. Dana-Gresen is run with the philosophy that the worker on the floor is the expert for his or her particular operation. Dana-Gresen management recognizes that the machine operator is often the best person to know what would improve that operation.

A natural response of employees to efforts such as EIM is to be suspicious of management motives. Workers wonder how many jobs will be eliminated by the "improved efficiencies." As a result, an organization must have the trust of the employees it expects to have implement the new order. Dana-Gresen employees were promised that jobs would not be eliminated as a result of EIM; layoffs would occur only because of major business fluctuations (Hinze 1993).

■ Reduced Cycle Times

Consistent with Shingo's (1992) philosophy, Dana-Gresen has focused considerable attention on reducing setup times. With many setups being reduced from several hours to a few minutes or eliminated altogether, the company has gained greater flexibility to meet customer needs. Dana-Gresen has improved its responsiveness to customers dramatically. Lead times that used to reach 26 weeks in 1986 have been reduced to four to six weeks.

■ Reduced Inventory Levels

Prior to EIM, 30% of the plant floor space was needed to store inventory in various stages of completion. By using EIM, the floor space occupied by inventory has declined to 15%. This improvement is due mainly to Dana-Gresen's nonstock-production policy and the placement of production components and supplies at the production cells. Each production cell stores its own inventory.

■ The Concept of "Customer"

The concept of customer has become a key concept across the plant. Customers are not only the entities to whom the company ships products but also internal entities that may rely on support from another unit within the plant. This broader definition allows every employee, value-added or nonvalue-added, to be customer driven.

The Changing Information-Reporting Landscape

■ Employee Empowerment — Accounting Impact

Since 1987 Dana-Gresen has pushed responsibility down to the cell level not only for operational decision making but also for data gathering and analysis. The purpose of this approach is to create ownership of the process and of the measurements. Ownership of the process will increase the chances that change will be successful. According to Neusiis (1993), if Dana-Gresen wants employees at the cell level to be concerned about on-time delivery and defect rates, the employees must be allowed to collect measurements, make them visible, and claim ownership for the results. This procedure works because employees now understand their system and where their measurements are coming from. In collecting and analyzing their own data, employees come to realize the complexity of the information system and to appreciate the work involved in gathering and reporting the data.

Because of reduced cycle time, production personnel need less information about work-in-process inventory. One of the benefits of JIT is that much of the intermediate accounting transaction processing is eliminated (Boncher 1993).

■ Changes in Report Generation

Formerly, the accounting function generated virtually all reports to the organization. Now, with tools such as the relational report generator, user departments can access the data directly themselves and produce reports in the needed formats. The information users keep their own scorecard out on the production floor. Work cells produce their own reports, typically Pareto graphs, that measure performance in productivity, quality, scrap, safety, and task/equipment certification. The workers prefer to generate their own numbers and are closer to them as a result (Hinze 1993).

One particular manufacturing cell collects its own information on defects generated within the cell. The cell tracks the source of the problem (for example: internal machining or supplier quality problems). At one point in 1991 the cell was running 47% scrap and linked the problem to materials defects from a particular supplier. The cell was able to work with the supplier to help identify where in the supplier's process the defect was occurring. In the past, chronic scrap problems might continue unchecked for long periods of time, until someone asked accounting to determine how much was being scrapped. With the present system, cell workers collect and track their own data and can immediately identify and correct systematic scrap problems (McDougall 1993).

■ Reducing Levels of Detail

Dana-Gresen has continually reexamined the usefulness of overly detailed data collection and reporting. Controller Roger Hinze relates:

> It wasn't long ago when every operation performed on the floor was recorded and measured against some engineering standard. The operator was spending a significant portion of his time just doing paperwork. Daily, weekly, and monthly reports were produced detailing each operation performed. These reports were determined to be nonvalue-added and were eliminated in favor of a simpler reporting scheme in which the cell manager reports total hours worked per employee, broken down as production time or meeting time.

■ Accounting for In-Process Inventories

Cycle times have been shortened to the point that generating transactions for intermediate transfers is not cost effective. During Hinze's tenure as controller, Dana-Gresen has elected not to track in-process inventories. Dana-Gresen uses a backflush approach in which materials are charged to inventory as they are received. Inventory is relieved of the cost of production materials when the product is completed and shipped. As Hinze says, "We are not in business to keep cost accountants employed; we are in business to service the customers and shareholders."

■ Eliminating Unused Reports

Plant Manager Tom Neusiis indicated that many unused accounting reports have been eliminated. Also, paper transfers were reduced and replaced by computerized data collection. An attempt has been made to "boil down" operating data into a few critical measurements rather than produce volumes of reports that generate marginal interest.

Hinze's experience indicates that a "back door" approach can be effective in reducing the volume of reports.

> Many unnecessary reports can be eliminated informally by simply "forgetting" to produce them. If the omission goes unnoticed, the report is apparently not being used. . . . This approach is more effective than simply asking the user if he or she needs the report, in which case the user will usually want to retain it.

■ Eliminating Rear-View Mirror Analysis

Dana-Gresen has moved away from detailed, backward-looking analyses. According to Neusiis, such analyses would require additional analytical staff yet not provide value to the customer. He believes that Dana-Gresen is better off because of this approach. In addition, delays are minimized because fewer decision makers are in the loop.

■ Communicating Operating Results to Employees

Dana-Gresen has made a significant attempt to make finance more easily understood by employees. Dana-Gresen holds monthly meetings with employees to present the latest financial results. In presenting financial information to employees, Dana-Gresen managers are careful not to use financial jargon without explaining what key financial terms mean (example: ROI).

Management Accounting: Doing More with Less

Dana-Gresen has experienced a remarkable reduction in full-time equivalent employees (FTE) in the areas of accounting and information systems since 1981. Exhibit 3-1 compares FTEs for 1993 with 1981. Although a few reductions occurred through layoffs, most FTE reductions can be attributed to the willingness of employees to absorb the responsibilities of departing employees, elimination of nonvalue-added tasks, and improved accounting efficiencies through computerization. Indeed, the culture within the controller's office encouraged motivated accounting employees to examine alternatives to additional FTEs.

Hinze tells of one of his staff accountants who asked him to delay

Exhibit 3-1. Minneapolis Plant—Accounting and Systems FTEs

	1981	*1993*
General accounting	11.0	2.7
Cost accounting	6.0	3.0
Credit and property	4.0	.3
Total accounting	21.0	6.0
Systems and EDP	11.0	3.0
Data processing	9.0	0.0
Total systems	20.0	3.0
Total accounting and systems	41.0	9.0

replacement of a departed employee. This accountant wanted to see if the duties could be reevaluated and the essential functions assumed by the remaining staff. As a result, several FTEs have been reabsorbed, reducing headcount from 21 in 1981 to six in 1993.

General Accounting and Budget Manager Aija Vijums emphasizes that the FTE reabsorption was accomplished without formal committee study, reporting, or fanfare. The accounting staff "just did it" (absorbed departed FTEs) as a matter of routine (Vijums 1993).

Similarly, the information systems headcount was reduced from 20 in 1981 to three in 1993. A decision to go with off-the-shelf manufacturing software (such as MAPICS) and minimize in-house custom programming made it possible virtually to eliminate the need for on-site programmers. Also gone are machine operators and data-entry clerks. Data are entered from the work cells and reports are requested directly from the computer by line personnel. What makes this transition even more remarkable is that the Minneapolis plant is processing data for two sister plants in addition to its own local operations.

The Dana-Gresen computer system is based on an IBM AS/400 running MAPICS integrated accounting software. The underlying accounting database tables are relational and ad hoc queries and reports can be generated through the relational report writer.

■ Off-the-Shelf Versus Custom Software

An attempt has been made at Dana-Gresen to avoid simply duplicating existing information systems functions when implementing new systems. When Dana-Gresen adopted MAPICS manufacturing accounting software, the general manager took the position that Dana-Gresen would not change the software to make it work like the previous system or to accommodate the way users were accustomed to working. Rather, users would have to reexamine their operating patterns and adjust them to be able to use the software (Gargano 1993).

While the off-the-shelf approach appears to conflict with traditional systems development wisdom (i.e., meeting the perceived needs of users), there are important practical considerations. First, users may not really know what they need. Moreover, what users think they need may simply reinforce their traditional methods and practices. As a result, the extra costs associated with the custom system bring few new benefits. Second, customized software complicates the process of regular vendor upgrades. When a company has invested significant time and resources to modify vendor software, each new release means that the customization must be redone to keep the software "backward compatible."

■ Custom Reporting Through Database Queries

While custom program changes have been minimal with the MAPICS manufacturing software, users can design custom queries that access the relational database maintained on the AS/400. This feature enables users to obtain reports not supplied by the turnkey system without requiring custom enhancements to the basic MAPICS code.

To use the query generator, a user must understand the file structures. In other words, the user must know which files contain the data being sought and the relationship among those files (such as linking fields). The user then can direct the query generator to retrieve data according to the desired conditions and generate output in a specified format (Gargano 1993).

Dana-Gresen Cost Accounting Manager Joe Lundell (1993) has been active in developing queries for additional analysis as well as serving as a consultant to departments outside accounting. He has assisted the personnel department and the production schedulers with query setup and has instructed them how to activate their query from their own terminals. Lundell suggests that line personnel could be trained to write their own queries but sees potential pitfalls. For example, an error in query design might produce a misleading report. He feels that accountants are more aware of control issues and system limitations than line personnel and are perhaps better trained to evaluate and test the queries.

Lundell has developed an impressive inventory of queries not only for accounting use but also for line personnel use. They include:

➤ Twenty-four-month customer sales history by part number,
➤ Four-week production requirement for "SP" cell,
➤ Excess inventory report,
➤ No usage report,
➤ Inventory value of purchase parts in stock,
➤ One-week production requirement for "relief" cell,
➤ Two-week production requirement for kit area,
➤ Monthly report of all cycle count adjustments,
➤ Percent of production done on work orders vs. kanban,
➤ Purchased parts with last usage of [date],
➤ Old manufacturing orders still open with last activity date prior to [date],
➤ Scrap reports for vendor and in-house.

In another query application, Dana-Gresen has eliminated paper transfers in some manufacturing cells. The researcher was shown one cell that had gone totally paperless with respect to filling shipping orders. The computer screen indicated how many units needed to be processed to meet current customer orders. By using a query developed by Lundell, the computer terminal located in the work cell accessed order information maintained on-line in the IBM AS/400 to determine how many additional units needed to be processed to meet shipment requirements for the day.

Activity-Based Management

Dana-Gresen prefers the concept of activity-based management (ABM) to that of activity-based costing (ABC). Lundell suggests that while ABC is useful in obtaining more accurate cost information, ABM goes a step beyond by allowing the management of activities, particularly nonvalue-added activities. Where ABC focuses on alternative overhead allocation bases, ABM focuses on the activities themselves. For example, an ABM system should identify the cost of issuing a purchase order. Because this is a nonvalue-added activity, the ABM system must give management the opportunity to affect the cost of this activity through improved efficiencies or, in some cases, elimination.

Among the findings from Dana-Gresen's initial ABM study were that some established product lines were more profitable than first thought. The change in the allocation basis for product engineering reflected that the established product required fewer engineering resources. Under previous overhead allocation schemes, engineering might be allocated according to direct labor hours and not accurately reflect the resources consumed by a particular product or activity.

■ Employee Perceptions of Their Activities

An important part of the ABM development process is meeting with cell personnel to determine what their major activities are as well as who their internal customers are. Typically, a manufacturing cell will perform three to five activities (an activity is recognized if it consumes more than 10% of the available time). Each activity is classified as being either value-added or nonvalue-added.

As one ABM interview was drawing to a close after having identified the major cell activities, one cell employee expressed concern that his work assignment was not represented among the cell activities. He was told that his work did not comprise more than 10% of the department's time and therefore his activity could not be included. When the employee persisted in his concerns, he was asked what his work assignment was. He responded that he moved materials, which the facilitator then added to the list of activities on the storyboard. When asked if his assignment was value-added or nonvalue-added, the employee replied that it was value-added. When the facilitator explained that moving materials is a nonvalue-added activity, the employee quipped, "Why don't you make that nonvalue-added when I retire next year!" (Lundell 1993).

■ Motivational Impact of ABM

ABM focuses attention on the fact that all activities performed within the plant, production and clerical alike, have cost consequences. As the costs of these activities are identified, ABM can indicate to the production worker the cost consequences of his or her decisions or actions.

While interviewing a work cell employee as part of an activity-based management project, Lundell pointed out that floor space is part of the product cost. During a follow-up visit, Lundell noticed that the cell configuration had been changed to free up space formerly occupied by inventory. According to the employees, they no longer needed the space because it was costing them money.

■ How Dana-Gresen will use ABM

The results from Dana-Gresen's ABM pilot study suggest some interesting possibilities. For example, the ABM project identified the costs of 106 activities performed throughout the plant. These individual activity costs can be used as a basis for benchmarking both inside and outside Dana-Gresen (Lundell 1993).

Because each activity is identified as being either value-added or nonvalue-added, waste can be eliminated by focusing on activities that do not benefit customers. In addition, the ABM system can help manufacturing cells see that some of their actions within the cell may generate nonvalue-added activities in other service departments. For example, Production Manager Tim Boncher would like to be able to measure the cost savings that would result if a part could be eliminated (as a result of common parts engineering). ABM would provide the cost of the activities needed to order and maintain an item of inventory, allowing design personnel to make more intelligent design decisions.

Finally, the results of ABM will yield more realistic cost structures by product line. Accounting can use this information to arrive at more accurate customer quotations.

Accounting Innovation and Improved Operations

Accountants at Dana-Gresen have had the unique opportunity to influence line operations, particularly in the area of inventory management. Innovations in the area of kanban management and inventory cycle counts are discussed in the following sections.

■ Kanban Cards–Merchandise Purchasing

Dana-Gresen uses a kanban system for many of its supplies and parts. A laminated kanban card contains prerecorded information about the part (part numbers, descriptions, standard quantity). It goes back and forth between Dana-Gresen and its suppliers, replacing the paper purchase order. Dana-Gresen is attempting to reduce ordering delays by having cell employees route the kanban card directly to the supplier, thus removing the purchasing step from the loop and giving cell workers more control over the timing of purchases. In addition to paper reduction, fewer purchasing errors, and shorter purchasing lead times, the system allows smaller inventories of parts and supplies to be kept on hand.

Lundell, as a member of the kanban committee, was instrumental in introducing improvements to Dana-Gresen's kanban system. One of the improvements introduced by the committee resulted in faster inventory cycle counts. Their approach calls for the manufacturing cells to set up their inventory to simplify the counting process. For example, loose pieces must be sealed in bags with standard counts such as 100 or 1,000. Only one bag is to be open at one time. As a result, the sealed bags can be counted rapidly. This approach eliminated the need to haul scales to weigh loose items stored in bins or other containers. Agreements have been reached with some suppliers to deliver supplies and component parts in easily countable lot sizes.

Similarly, machined in-process parts can be counted more easily with the use of standard-count baskets or trays. The trays are designed with slots for a standard count that will facilitate cycle counting. For example, a tray may have slots for 50 units (or another such easily counted number). The slots make it easy for the cycle counter either to determine that the tray is full and record the standard count or to count a partially filled tray quickly.

■ Inventory Cycle Counts

Lundell relates that inventory cycle counts originated when a cell manager asked him what he had to do to avoid having to take a full physical inventory. Lundell provided standards for accuracy of cycle counts as well as guidelines for their frequency. Several manufacturing cells have qualified their cycle-counting systems and are thus exempted from full physical inventory.

Accounting Measures of Quality and Productivity

Consistent with Dana-Gresen's philosophy of employee empowerment, most quality and productivity measures are gathered and analyzed by line personnel. As with other manufacturing cells and support departments, the management accounting function measures its own productivity in such areas as responsiveness to customer quotation requests. Prominently displayed Pareto graphs in color show how quickly customers receive quotation responses from accounting (most are completed within one day). Similarly, credit memorandums are analyzed by month by source of error with the largest errors being highlighted.

■ Plantwide Quality and Productivity Measures

On a monthly basis, accounting measures *production per equivalent plant employee*. This measure is intended to keep track of the productivity of hours actually worked and remove distortions caused by vacation time, holiday time, and sick leave being included in total salaries. Production per equivalent plant employee looks only at the actual hours worked and divides it by 173.3 hours (2,080 annual hours divided by 12 months) to arrive at the equivalent number of plant employees. Total sales dollars produced for the month then are divided by the equivalent number of plant employees to arrive at production per equivalent plant employee.

Accounting also produces a quality cost summary detailing expenditures for defect prevention, quality appraisal, internal failures and rework, and rework due to external failures. While these measures still generate interest from various parties external to Dana-Gresen (quality auditors, ISO 9000 certification, etc.), Neusiis questions the effectiveness of cost of quality as a tool for employee motivation. He suggests that it is not a very responsive measure and changes slowly over time. (Neusiis compares the usefulness of this measure to tracking the interest rate on a home mortgage; it has probably not changed in several years.) Employees do not see their actions as having an effect on this measure, and thus it loses much of its motivating power. He suggests that managers should follow this measure over the long run and not get overly excited about it in the short run.

Implications of the Dana-Gresen Experience

1. The EIM culture must permeate the accounting function. It is noteworthy at Dana-Gresen that the EIM culture permeates the accounting function as well as the production area. Just as individual production cells strive for continuous improvement and to reduce setup times and eliminate nonvalue-added activities, accounting reaches corresponding objectives in the area of information services. At Dana-Gresen this task has been accomplished by eliminating unused reports and other nonvalue-added activities and by serving the organization with a much smaller head count.

2. *Manufacturing cells must be empowered not only to affect their own operations but also to gather, analyze, and be responsible for their own measures.* The empowerment of the manufacturing cells has important implications for the accounting function. Where accounting used to be the only scorekeeper, data are now gathered and analyzed at the cell level. This is as it should be because workers know their operations and the proper measures needed to control those operations. Furthermore, the cell now owns the information and will be inclined to take responsibility for the resulting measures. This is consistent with the idea that accounting information should not drive operations (Johnson 1992).

3. *Accounting may find itself more detached from the "operational loop."* The push-down of much of the data gathering and analysis may extend to such areas as purchasing and inventory management. Using the kanban card approach as Dana-Gresen does, cells may short-circuit the purchasing/acquisition cycle by sending the precoded kanban card directly to the supplier. This method may reduce the traditional involvement of accounting in the acquisition cycle.

4. *Management accountants must avail themselves of modern database tools.* Modern database technology provides many opportunities for the accountant to provide value-added services for internal customers. For example, the increasing use of relational databases along with sophisticated report and query generators allows more access than ever before to the data stored in the system. However, accountants must be knowledgeable about the data structures and the available query tools to gain access to the data. The accounting function at Dana-Gresen has taken a leadership role in the use of this technology and thereby has gained additional stature in the organization through higher levels of customer service.

5. *Shorter cycle times will require less-detailed transaction analysis.* The high volumes of transaction data required to track products through various stages of production become less relevant as production cycle times decrease. In many cases, transaction processing lags significantly behind actual product movement, resulting in untimely and therefore useless reports. In addition, time spent by plant employees recording such transactions is nonvalue-added. More practical accounting approaches such as the backflush must be developed to simplify transaction processing in this environment.

6. Accounting must develop a customer service orientation. Accountants may not view their contribution as being value-added from an external customer perspective. Nevertheless, accountants must identify their internal customers and seek to satisfy them just as the manufacturing cells try to satisfy the external customers. Dana-Gresen has been particularly successful in this area despite their small staff. The Dana-Gresen accounting staff has excelled in communicating financial and operating results to employees and educating them to understand the significance of key financial measures. They also have provided additional reporting capabilities to both management and production areas through the use of modern database technology. Their pilot ABM study has shed important light on the cost structures of key activities throughout the plant, and their innovations in the area of inventory management, such as cycle counting and kanban, have led to improvements in cell productivity.

Conclusion

The accounting function at Dana-Gresen may well be a prototype for the next generation of management accountants. They have embraced the philosophy of EIM by eliminating waste and enhancing internal customer support while reducing accounting and information systems FTEs. This department has been innovative in its use of modern database technology to increase the quality and scope of its own operations and to provide valuable information to manufacturing cells. Also, its ambitious ABM study has played a key role in identifying key plant activities and the relationship of these activities to product cost.

References

Boncher, T. 1993. Production manager, Dana-Gresen. On-site interview, June 10-11.

Gargano, G. 1993. MIS manager, Dana-Gresen. On-site interview, June 10-11.

Hinze, R. 1993. Controller-sales administration, Dana-Gresen. On-site interview, June 10-11.

Johnson, H.T. 1992. *Relevance Regained.* New York: The Free Press, a division of Macmillan, Inc.

Lundell, J. 1993. Cost accounting manager, Dana-Gresen. On-site interview, June 10-11.

McDougall, R. 1993. Excellence in manufacturing coordinator, Dana-Gresen. On-site interview, June 10-11.

Neusiis, T. 1993. Plant manager, Dana-Gresen. On-site interview, June 10-11.

Vijums, A. 1993. General accounting and budget manager, Dana-Gresen. On-site interview, June 10-11.

Shingo, S. 1992. *Shigeo Shingo: The Shingo Production Management System* (translated by Andrew P. Dillon).. Cambridge, Massachusetts: Productivity Press, Inc.

4

Information Support for a World-Class Manufacturer

Proactive Management Accounting at Iomega Corporation

Introduction

Iomega Corporation, located in Roy, Utah, is a leading manufacturer of removable computer storage devices. Founded in 1980, the company went public in 1983 and presently employs 1,600 people in its worldwide operations. The company has weathered some difficult times, particularly in 1987 when it experienced a $36 million loss on sales of less than $90 million. However, under new management and with a new focus on total quality control (TQC) and manufacturing cost reduction, the company has returned to profitability.

A cultural change within the company was engineered by top management based on concepts from Goldratt and Fox (1984) and Deming (1986). Iomega has devoted significant resources to training employees in quality, productivity, and customer satisfaction efforts. Of particular note is the extensive use of self-directed work teams. Iomega's commitment to improvements in production methodologies and customer focus earned them The Shingo Prize for Excellence in American Manufacturing for 1992.

Proactive Management Accounting Support

The management accounting (MA) role in the evolution of Iomega toward world-class status in manufacturing both inside and outside the

MA department is characterized as a supporting one. Although MA did not lead this transition, many innovations leading toward world-class manufacturing were greatly influenced by former accountants.

It is interesting to note that the accounting perspective has been unusually influential in the operational areas of Iomega. For example, former controller John Thompson is presently vice president of manufacturing. Furthermore, the cost accounting function had until recently been physically housed adjacent to manufacturing until space limitations forced them to be relocated to the finance area. Cost analysts are assigned to major product components. Through a process of *career broadening* they come to understand the manufacturing process. Analysts have been known to work so closely with line personnel that they have come to have conflicting loyalties between the finance department and the line personnel.

Costing innovations such as activity-based costing were driven by high-level production leaders such as Thompson, the former controller. The CFO suggests that resistance might have resulted if such programs came from accounting rather than from the production area (Krumb 1993).

Nevertheless, MA views their contributions such as *flexible budgeting* and producing *actual product costs* on a monthly basis as having provided critically needed support for production. MA also has acted as a "challenger," questioning the need for certain data collection and reporting and making sure that the "right" activities are being tracked. Moreover, MA has provided this support with a stable or declining head count.

Management Accounting Involvement in Modern Production Approaches and Technologies

■ Total Quality Control

The MA function has assisted in the TQC movement as members of teams or as team facilitators. The quality teams cross functional boundaries. TQC also has been employed within the MA function itself to improve processes and maintain or reduce head count. Freed-up resources from nonvalue-added activities such as collections and purchasing can be redirected toward more proactive uses of accounting resources.

For example, the finance department assembled a TQC team to perform a housecleaning of the chart of accounts. The goal was to reduce the 600,000 accounts being maintained at that time on computer to an active subset of accounts that would result in significant savings in computer processing time at month-end closing time. In addition, the clean set of accounts would be easier to understand and would result in fewer coding errors. Results of this TQC activity were that the published chart of accounts was reduced from 38 pages to 15 pages. The total number of valid account combinations was reduced from 600,000 to 180,000 records, thus reducing database disk space by 70%.

Another TQC team was formed to increase productivity on accounts payable processing. Prior to this TQC activity, purchase invoices were routed back to the requisitioning department for approval prior to payment. In reviewing compiled statistics for such approvals the team discovered that very few of the invoices were ever disputed, so in the vast majority of cases, this step did not add value to the process. The old procedure was replaced by a "negative approval" process in which a photocopy of the invoice was sent to the department with a stamped notation indicating that this invoice would be paid unless the requisitioning department notified the accounts payable department otherwise.

A TQC team found ways to streamline the month-end closing to free up more time for proactive and value-added tasks as well as to make operating results available on a more timely basis. The team reduced time spent on adjusting entries by limiting the entries made for immaterial amounts. The team identified several employees whose time spent on the closing represented a bottleneck to the process. Steps were taken to cover or eliminate duties for these persons that did not relate to the closing. Redundant financial statement reviews were consolidated.

■ Just-in-Time Manufacturing

While Iomega does not use classic JIT, there has been a significant focus on reducing cycle times, particularly on reducing supplier lead times. If supplier lead times are reduced, buffer stocks can be reduced and the production process can be more reactive to customer demands.

Cycle-time reduction. The inability of marketing to predict product sales led to conflicts between the sales and production functions. This prediction difficulty stems mainly from the multitiered distribution system in which Iomega sells to distributors, who sell to retailers, who sell to end-users. In some situations value-added retailers (consultants) add an additional tier. In addressing this perennial problem, former CEO Fred Wenninger pointed out that if demand for the product cannot be predicted accurately, Iomega must concentrate on reducing cycle time to focus on meeting individual orders as they are received.

Engineering change flexibility. The focus on cycle-time reduction also has necessitated new thinking about strategies for cost reduction. In addition to material and component costs, Iomega's MA team must consider factors such as the cost of obsolescence and the degree of needed flexibility to react to engineering changes. This is termed "total cost of ownership" and encompasses cycle time, quality, flexibility, and support costs—not just purchase cost.

Iomega illustrates the application of this concept by choosing to buy integrated circuits from a local manufacturer, even though overseas suppliers offer lower prices. However, when the cost of obsolescence and/or engineering changes is taken into account the locally produced components lead to lower overall costs. For example, if a design change is necessary involving reprogramming of the chips, a call can be made to the local manufacturer to stop its production run and prepare for an engineering change that will arrive in the afternoon. The local manufacturer can deliver the new circuits the next day. Because of the responsiveness of this arrangement, little scrap (perhaps a half-day's worth) results from the design change.

■ Fixed and Variable Costs

Despite widespread criticism of the approach, Iomega still employs an analysis of fixed and variable costs. According to Tom Kerber, the director of operating financial controls at Iomega, flexible variable costs can be made more efficient. With short-term fixed costs such as payroll, the company's only options are to lay an employee off or decline to hire the employee initially. In the case of fixed assets, the company can dispose of a building, but only in the long term. Fixed cost control involves high-level management action and a longer period of time to take effect. Kerber prefers that manufacturing people focus on the costs they can control—the variable costs (Kerber 1993). The director of central financial for Iomega, Dan Strong, adds that a bid should be accepted if variable costs can be covered. This makes the variable cost analysis relevant. Iomega also looks at variable costs below the gross margin line (variable expenses associated with distribution) (Strong 1993).

MA Support of Other Functional Departments

The management accounting function appears to be highly respected within Iomega. Accounting expertise is sought regularly to support product cost analysis and product pricing. The MA function is regularly represented on cross-functional quality teams. High-level managers, for example the VP of manufacturing, ask if accounting has validated key data being used as decision inputs. One problem with relying on cost data produced by an engineer on the line is that engineering cost perspectives are in many cases too narrow. The engineer may forget to consider costs such as overhead, obsolescence, and warranty costs that do not appear on the bill of materials. The accountant possesses a broader concept of product cost.

■ Marketing

The support provided by MA in marketing is primarily in the area of product pricing. Kerber suggests that MA does not so much provide support as exercise control. The MA function maintains tight control over the latitude that sales personnel have in pricing products. Nonstandard pricing must be approved by accounting. Marketing personnel generally view this control positively; they appreciate the assurance that their pricing decisions will not hurt the company.

■ Productivity Measurement

MA saw the labor productivity report as a nonvalue-added activity and eliminated it. The main reason for this action is the fact that labor costs represent only 5% to 10% of total product cost. Approximately 420 positions, out of 900 total employees, are considered direct labor, and less than 20% of all salary and wages is considered direct labor. As a result, the labor efficiency variances presented in the labor productivity report were considered not only irrelevant but having the potential to contribute to incentives inconsistent with the "pull" concept adopted by Iomega. Iomega has determined that other more timely and effective methods exist for managing direct labor.

■ Customer Satisfaction

The MA function monitors key indicators of customer satisfaction such as warranty costs, stock rotation, and customer returns (credit memorandums). MA views credit memorandums as avoidable errors. According to this view, either a mistake was made by Iomega personnel in shipping the wrong types or amounts of product, or the customer has caused the error in its ordering process.

The company has taken action through their TQC program to reduce the nonvalue-added activity of reconciling customer accounts receivable adjustments. It was noted at Iomega that too much time was being spent cleaning up errors in accounts rather than in collecting receivables. It was delaying the collection of receivables. The team determined that collecting a receivable became more difficult if the account was littered with sundry debit and credit memos, indicating that portions of the amounts owed were in dispute. A TQC team was assembled to track the number of credit memos and the source of the errors. Other customer service measurements tracked by MA include the costs, duration, and wait time of customer service calls.

■ Product Quality

Accounting measures of product quality include tracking warranty costs and maintaining warranty reserves as well as computing the cost of scrap. The latter measure is an indication of the quality of the in-process product.

■ Motivation of Departmental Managers

Activity-based costing at Iomega has proved to be a powerful tool for providing incentives to lower the consumption of overhead and allow (at least in the longer term) for the reduction of both fixed and variable product costs. The finance department has implemented activity-based methodology in the area of overhead cost allocation. They are moving toward an allocation technology in which managers actually can reduce the allocation of costs to their department by reducing their demand for such services.

Formerly, a fixed CIS budget line-item was assigned to each functional department. Although this amount was subject to negotiation up front, managers essentially viewed it as an allocation that they could not control. The new approach attempts to assign CIS costs on the basis of usage as captured by cost drivers such as "CPU minutes." Managers realize that they can reduce their CIS allocation by reducing the minutes of CPU time used. Similarly, the communications department costs are allocated based on the number of phone lines in the department, so a department manager can reduce such allocations by eliminating unneeded phone capacity.

Allocating plant overhead based on square footage occupied has been very effective at Iomega to reduce the space used. This method also has given additional incentives to cut back on the size of WIP inventories to conserve space.

In the above instances, it is important to note that while charges to operating departments are lowered by reduced consumption, the total overhead may remain constant in the short term. However, these short-term incentives eventually translate into long-term overhead pool reductions. For example, Iomega eliminated the need for two manufacturing buildings through this incentive.

Allowing outside competition to functional departments has appeared to be a driving force in the adoption of TQC and cycle-time reduction methodologies. Departments that previously had difficulty reducing costs suddenly had tremendous incentive to eliminate nonvalue-added costs when faced with outside competition. The magnetic recording head department formerly occupied an entire building within the Iomega production complex. This department was under pressure to get costs down and essentially was threatened with outsourcing. The department manager determined that he could cut his space cost in half by reconfiguring his production line so that it occupied one-half of the original space. While the space cost allocation was reduced for this department, lease expense for the entire building continued in the short term. Eventually, however, other space reconfigurations allowed Iomega to stop leasing an entire building.

■ Monitoring Key Production Activities

Responsibility for monitoring is distributed across the organization. MA tracks financially relevant metrics, such as the number of completions and units of production.

■ Daily Chart

The finance department designed the initial version of the daily chart, a one-page compilation of Pareto analyses for key operating indicators. The chart allows high-level executives within Iomega to keep a finger on the pulse of operations.

Outside Views of Management Accounting

■ Production Scheduling

An interesting view of Iomega's management accounting function was obtained from Catherine Muniz, director of materials control, a former cost accounting manager who was reassigned to production scheduling. Muniz and the manufacturing team installed the visual kanbans to affect the pull system.

Although Muniz views the work done by accounting as pivotal in the costing area, she feels strongly that the measurement and analysis of data should be done by those who own the process, not by MA. For example, if her department needs a particular issue analyzed, she feels that her department would be the logical choice for producing and analyzing the data. This way she can prioritize such analytical activities. If such responsibilities are reassigned to accounting, their priorities may not be the same as in production scheduling. Moreover, such data collection and analysis requires specialized operational knowledge. For example, production scheduling has developed systems and procedures to analyze obsolescence, product phaseout, detail inventory analysis, transportation, and importation costs. According to Muniz, scheduling department data are geared to a specific decision or action or to affirm some action that has already been taken. She believes accounting is too far outside the loop and not involved closely enough in the day-to-day decisions (Muniz 1993).

As an example, an internal audit revealed that import duties on some imported components and materials were overpaid. The problem was very difficult to track because line-item detail on duty paid was not available in the system. Production scheduling had to rekey part numbers, quantities, and invoice prices on imported items. Duty rates vary by item. Muniz had a database system developed to track the items subject to duty. The result has been the identification of an additional overhead pool. The payoff for this system was that a $300,000 refund was obtained from U.S. Customs.

It is interesting to note that the production scheduling department is now providing accounting with per-unit freight and duty information that they will use in their actual cost analysis. In addition to tracking duty rates, they have implemented a duty drawback program that uses information from the import database along with export information to file for U.S. Customs refunds. This program uses management accounting techniques to analyze large volumes of data and maintain necessary audit trails.

This decentralized approach to decision support is consistent with Iomega's emphasis on team and employee empowerment. The empowerment concept allows responsibility to be pushed outward (Johnson 1992). The CFO endorses this concept and believes that people need to feel responsible for supplying their own data needs within their own functional departments (Krumb 1993).

According to Muniz, Iomega has reduced the number of degreed people in accounting. As Iomega moved toward process improvement, the growth in degreed people with business analytical skills has grown in operations.

■ Manufacturing

The vice president for manufacturing at Iomega views the contribution of MA in the area of activity-based costing to be of great value to the organization in arriving at more cost-effective designs (Thompson 1993). Thompson suggests that product designs often do not take into account the true costs of an overly complex design. For example, a design might call for 10 capacitors rather than one multipurpose capacitor because the sum of the 10 individual components is less than the cost of the single component. The engineer does not account, however, for the overhead costs associated with purchasing and stocking the many "inexpensive" components. Thompson believes that MA improves product design by identifying the additional cost drivers associated with the effort to maintain a larger variety of parts.

Future Directions for Management Accounting at Iomega

■ Proactive Management Accounting

The finance department at Iomega has developed a values statement to guide its operations. The four major principles are: commitment to our (finance) people, fiduciary and fiscal responsibility, service orientation, and proactivity. The finance constituents are called *partners*. Of particular note is the principle of proactivity. The finance department is committed to providing service to its partners by giving them information they are not aware they need. The values statement is reproduced in Exhibit 4-1.

■ Emphasis on Reduced Cycle Times

The CFO at Iomega suggests that a major change having an impact on accountants is that schedule (cycle time) has become more important from a financial standpoint than cost is. Although predicting future sales remains problematic, short cycle times allow the company to react quickly to sales orders. Also, they reduce the costs associated with work-in-process. Short cycle times also reduce risks of product obsolescence and ongoing engineering changes. The CFO points out that it is more dangerous to inventory finished goods in anticipation of product orders than it is to inventory excess raw materials, mainly due to the obsolescence and engineering change factors (Krumb 1993).

■ Future-Oriented Management Accounting

Within the finance department, it is important that more time be spent planning for future activities than critiquing past operations. For example, with Iomega's Floptical product, considerable time is spent studying the cost structures in support of pricing strategies. Of particular importance are reasonable predictions of cost structures and pricing 12 months into the future.

■ Design-to-Cost

Strong points out that while Iomega spends a lot of time with costs in the manufacturing stage, little has been done to date with costs in the design stage. He suggests that 85% of the cost is designed into the product. This fact offers management accounting a significant opportunity to affect product costs at early phases in product development.

■ Elimination of Monthly Close Procedures

Iomega's MA department envisions an accounting systems environment in which key operating data, presently available only after the month-end close, are available daily or continuously. This commitment will re-

Exhibit 4-1. Iomega Corporation: Finance Department Values

- ■ Commitment to Our People

The people of Finance are our most important resource and the core of our service. In order to fully develop and trust each other, we must communicate with loyalty, openness, respect, and recognition. Each individual is empowered with the tools and authority to do their job in the manner they deem best. Personal accountability is expected and creativity is encouraged. Only through this environment will each individual and the whole Finance Department maximize their potential, both individually and collectively.

- ■ Fiduciary and Fiscal Responsiility

We have a responsibility to provide financial information in accordance with all accounting principles and legal regulations, such as GAAP, SEC, tax compliance, etc. We should behave in a manner which promotes actions which assure the assets of the company are utilized in the best manner possible.

- ■ Service Oriented

Finance is a service organization. Our job is to provide our partners with the information necessary for them to accomplish their objectives. This should complement our fiduciary and fiscal responsibility. We should act as a member of our partner's team.

- ■ Proactive

Part of providing service to our partners is giving them information they didn't know they needed. A proactive approach is paramount to giving the best possible service. Not all new ideas will result in ongoing processes, procedures or reports. However, all new ideas should be explored and applauded.

quire a more systematic approach to booking material accounting accruals with minimal human intervention. This approach will then be consistent with Iomega's forward-looking accounting philosophy.

■ Breaking from the Old MA Paradigm

The MA team emphasized the importance of questioning old habits of thought and breaking from outdated paradigms. Accounting procedures that fail to add value to firm operations or are no longer relevant in light of modern technology should be discarded. Iomega's internal auditor questions why a purchase invoice should be marked "paid" (Wesselman 1993). He argues that the computer already tracks paid invoices and would prevent a duplicate payment.

As the result of a TQC team activity in the fixed-asset area, accounting departed from traditional internal control wisdom calling for fixed-asset tagging. The team initially was concerned that too much time was being spent on nonvalue-added activities rather than on asset-management activities. One outgrowth of this TQC activity was the elimination of fixed-asset tagging. The rationale was that it was a time-consuming process that did not add value because inventoriable fixed assets have serial numbers that can be recorded in the fixed-asset database. The team concluded that the asset tag provided neither additional security nor enhanced tracking capability.

Implications for Management Accounting

1. Total quality must extend beyond manufacturing and into the accounting function. The excellence achieved at Iomega has resulted from a company-wide commitment to total quality both in manufacturing processes and support services. Iomega has shown that as a service department, MA must continually reexamine its processes to eliminate nonvalue-added activities and refocus its resources on proactive support of the goals of the organization. Iomega is an excellent example of how the accounting function can apply TQC principles to enhance its value to the organization.

2. Management accounting systems must adjust to modern manufacturing realities. Iomega demonstrates that the MA function must adjust to modern manufacturing environments to remain viable. Increased emphasis on reduced cycle times and smaller batch sizes at Iomega has changed traditional cost-analysis wisdom. Clearly, MA practice within the modern factory must facilitate the removal of constraints to achieving the broader goals of the company rather than emphasize efficiency within individual units.

3. *As manufacturing cells are empowered, more data collection and analyses will occur at the cell level rather than in the management accounting function.* Critics of management accounting such as Johnson (1992) emphasize that information from systems designed to enforce fiscal responsibility should not be used to control operations. It should be noted that information used for operational control at Iomega is generally collected and analyzed at the point where operational decisions are made, an example being the production scheduling department (Muniz 1993). However, this method does not remove responsibility from MA for ensuring that data collection methods and analytical methodology have integrity. It is noteworthy at Iomega that accounting often is called on to verify analyses prepared by other departments. It is in this capacity that MA has an opportunity to assist line operations directly in improving the quality of decision inputs.

The empowerment of work teams and the diffusion of data collection and analysis have some interesting implications for management accounting education. Muniz advocates moving more analytical business skills to the operational level. Doing so tends to cloud the distinction between management accounting functions and line functions, at least with respect to data gathering and analysis. The management accounting profession and their colleagues in higher education need to clarify the evolving role of management accounting in relationship to concepts such as team empowerment and broaden their students' perspectives on career paths and the contributions they can make to an organization.

4. *The placement of management accountants in manufacturing roles may be an effective way to enhance communications between accounting and production and increase MA credibility.* It appears that much of the success and stature of the MA function at Iomega is due to the placement of former accounting personnel in operating positions. The Muniz case suggests that accounting skills can lead to a successful career in an operating position. First, accountants generally possess well-developed analytical skills. Second, they understand the principles of cost accounting and the financial impact of operations. Third, they are able to communicate effectively with the accounting function. Finally, an accountant recognizes the limitations of cost accounting data and is able to identify areas and implement changes where data collection could be reduced or eliminated according to its usefulness and accuracy (Muniz 1993).

Conclusion

The management accounting function at Iomega has shown how the principles of TQC and continuous improvement can be used within a finance or accounting organization to eliminate nonvalue-added activities and redeploy accounting resources in a more proactive fashion. Management accounting must continue to question all its information support activities for relevance in light of the changing manufacturing environment. Accountants must not insulate themselves from the manufacturing realities of the organization or the customer. As Iomega has shown, accounting personnel can make the transition successfully from finance to manufacturing and gain a better perspective from which to support the operations of the firm.

References

Deming, W.E. 1986. *Out of the Crisis*. Cambridge, Massachusetts: MIT Center for Advanced Engineering Studies.

Goldratt, E.M., and Cox, J. 1984. *The Goal: Excellence in Manufacturing*. New York: North River Press, Inc.

Johnson, H.T. 1992. *Relevance Regained*. New York: The Free Press, a division of Macmillan, Inc.

Kerber, T. 1993. Director, operating financial controls, Iomega Corporation. On-site interview, March 22.

Krumb, P. 1993. Chief financial officer, Iomega Corporation. On-site interview, March 22.

Muniz, C. 1993. Director, materials control, Iomega Corporation. On-site interview, March 22.

Strong, D. 1993. Director, central financial, Iomega Corporation. On-site interview, March 22.

Thompson, J. 1993. Vice president, manufacturing, Iomega Corporation. Phone interview, April 28.

Wesselman, B. 1993. Manager, internal audit, Iomega Corporation. On-site interview, March 22.

5

Accounting Support of Total Quality Management Concepts
Wilson Sporting Goods Company

Introduction

Wilson Sporting Goods Co. (Wilson) has been manufacturing and marketing golf, baseball, basketball, and football equipment and other sporting goods for well over three-quarters of a century. It was organized in 1913 and began operations in Chicago. In 1970 Pepsico acquired Wilson and held it until 1985 when it was sold to Wesray. Wesray sold Wilson to its present owner, Amer of Finland, in 1989.

The Humboldt, Tennessee, plant is one of several Wilson manufacturing sites and is the subject of this report. This 182,000-square-foot plant is Wilson's only golf ball manufacturing facility at the present time. It was founded in 1977 and originally made rubber and leather basketballs and cut the leather for softballs. In 1982-83, a limited number of golf balls were produced. In 1984, 300,000 dozen were produced, and by 1985 the manufacture of rubber and leather basketballs was phased out and golf balls became the plant's sole production. In 1993, 580 employees operated three shifts a day for five days a week to provide annual production of approximately 100 million golf balls—17% of the market share. Manufacturing improvements are illustrated by the statistical information in Exhibit 5-1.

The production improvements shown in Exhibit 5-1 are rewarded by increased customer orders. The information shown in Exhibit 5-2 illustrates customer satisfaction by the increased orders and suggests that decreased lead times are partially responsible. While orders have increased from 6,232 in 1986 to 20,099 in 1993, the average lead time has dropped from 5.2 weeks to 1.8 weeks.

Exhibit 5-1. Summary of Manufacturing Measurements

Year	1985	1986	1987	1988	1989	1990	1991	1992	1993
Market share	2%	4%	7%	9%	12%	14%	17%	18%	19%
Employees	165	250	287	329	490	460	543	557	581
Budget (millions)	6.5	14.8	17.1	22.8	32.2	44.7	46.2	48.4	49.8
Output per associate (dozen balls)	547	760	865	1,100	1,195	981	1,210	1,222	1,153
Scrap savings (thousands)	Base year	72	64	235	256	280	467	526	593
Rework savings (thousands)	Base year	92	224	423	576	504	701	783	872
Inventory turns	6	10	16	30	59	65	80	83	86
Special order shipments	3,500	6,232	12,887	17,362	21,264	21,365	25,696	25,639	20,099
Late shipments	293	449	144	0	44	51	18	13	10
On-time shipments	92%	93%	98%	100%	99.80%	99.80%	99.90%	99.95%	99.95%
Lead time (days)	75	65	50	15	15	10	10 or less	Less than 10	Less than 10

Exhibit 5-2. Special Order Activity

Total Order (000) — Average Lead Time (weeks)

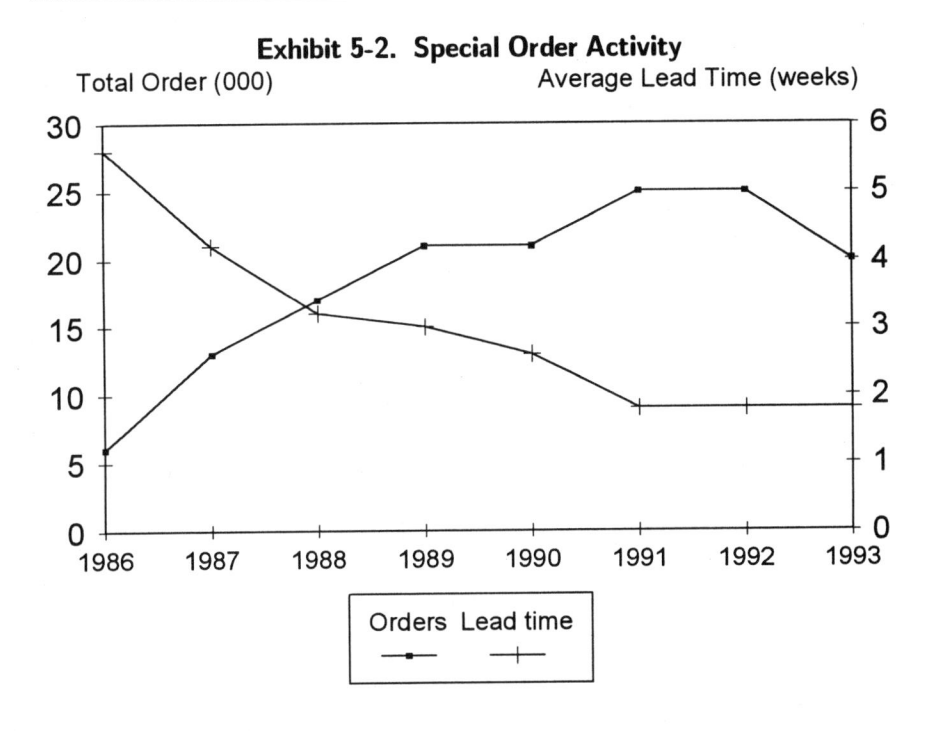

[Chart showing Orders decreasing from ~28 in 1986 to ~10 in 1991-1993, and Lead time increasing from ~1 in 1986 to ~5 in 1991-1992, dropping to ~4 in 1993, across years 1986–1993]

Management Support of Total Quality Management Concepts

Al Scott, the plant manager, joined Wilson in 1985. With the support of top management at corporate headquarters, Scott formulated the golf division's primary mission—to be a world-class factory with a world-class product. To achieve this mission it was necessary to revise the mission/vision statement to reflect the focus on quality and productivity. Exhibit 5-3 shows the revised statement.

Since the adoption of this mission/vision statement there has been continuous improvement in manufacturing at the Humboldt plant. This manufacturing excellence was recognized in October 1992 when *Industry Week* selected Wilson as one of 10 businesses named "America's Best." Wilson received an additional special recognition in April 1993 when it was selected as the large business recipient of the Shingo Prize for Excellence in Manufacturing.

Key to Wilson's continuous improvement has been its team efforts. In January 1987, when plan implementation began, there were three or four teams. Today there are over 40 formal teams that involve more than 85% of Wilson's employees. When informal teams are considered, employee participation in continuous improvement is 100%. The teams normally meet weekly but may meet bi-weekly or monthly depending on the nature of the problems addressed. A team may be dissolved if it is deemed that the efforts expended are greater than the rewards. This usually happens when some major problem has been solved or improvements have been made in a process so that further effort will provide only minimal rewards.

To help build a team atmosphere and break down the authoritarian approach to management, no members of management wear suits or ties. Instead, the members of management and other supervisors are called coaches and wear casual clothing. Because Wilson's product is golf balls, management's first choice of clothing is golf shirts with unique decorative logos that identify them as members of a specific team.

To further remove the authoritarian approach to management, the management team adopted a facilitator attitude. Several times each year, at special occasions such as Christmas, Thanksgiving, and Easter, the production teams bring their favorite dishes of food to share with their teammates. Members of management volunteered to operate the critical bottleneck machinery during the dinners. This gesture

Exhibit 5-3. Revised Mission/Vision Statement

Our Mission is to become the biggest and the best golf ball manufacturer/special order facility worldwide and to be recognized as such by our suppliers, customers, consumers, and competitors. This objective can only be obtained by becoming a world-class manufacturer. The guiding philosophies in our pursuit of world-class manufacturing are:

- Continuous-improvement processes
- Associate involvement
- Just-in-time
- Total quality management
- Lowest total cost manufacturer

The successful integration of these philosophies will result in the following:

- Superior associates—the highest competitive advantage
- Superior products via design and performance
- Superior manufacturing process capabilities and quality
- Superior customer satisfaction and service

(Wilson Sporting Goods Co., 1993 Shingo Prize—Excellence in Manufacturing, Application, p.3)

Wilson Sporting Goods Company

has brought respect and goodwill from the production team members toward management while giving the management members a greater understanding of the manufacturing process and respect for the production team.

To help focus on team assignments, management has encouraged each team to adopt a name descriptive of that team's assignment or goal. Some colorful names are Precision Painters for the team that affixes logos to special orders; Mr. Goodwrench for the machinery maintenance team; and Dust Busters for the clean workplace environment team. See Exhibit 5-4 for a list of the teams at Wilson as well as their meeting schedules.

Empowerment of teams to make decisions is crucial to their effectiveness. Wilson has empowered each team to spend up to $500 for any project that fits within company guidelines. These projects generally relate to quality, productivity, customer satisfaction, safety, and housekeeping.

To give visibility to the work and decisions of teams and to let others see what is being accomplished, the minutes of each team meeting are posted on bulletin boards. This posting of minutes keeps all employees of Wilson informed, creates a serious attitude on the part of all teams and team members, and builds a team spirit across functional lines that reduces ambivalence and jealousy.

Integrated into the team training at Wilson is the use of tools of TQM such as cause-and-effect diagrams, flow charts, histograms, Pareto analysis, and so forth. Teams and associates have been trained to use these tools to build quality into their processes. For example, the Dust Buster team was concerned with downtime. To solve this problem, a TQM data center was set up to supply the following information:

- A downtime chart,
- A downtime cause-and-effect diagram,
- A downtime Pareto chart,
- A quality control (QC) hold chart,
- A QC hold Pareto,
- An internal customer-complaints Pareto, and
- Absenteeism and safety charts.

The downtime chart showed the percentage of downtime of the total hours worked each month. It communicated the opportunities for improvement. The team used the cause-and-effect diagram and Pareto chart to show causes for the downtime. This information was used at the internal-customer meeting with maintenance to develop an action plan that reduced the downtime.

Exhibit 5-4. Team Wilson Meeting Room Schedules

Day	Time	Team	Room
Monday	12:45 am	Precision Painters	(Team Wilson Room A)
	3:00 am	Perfection Connection	(Team Wilson Room A)
	8:30 am	Materials Dept.	(Team Wilson Room A)
	1:00 pm	Mr. Goodwrench	(Team Wilson Room A)
	2:00 pm	Sidewinders	(Team Wilson Room A)
	9:30 pm	Midnight Molders	(Team Wilson Room A)
	10:00 pm	Rubber Roasters	(Team Wilson Room B)
	10:30 pm (1)	Midnight Safety	(Team Wilson Room A)
	11:00 pm	P.M. Molders	(Team Wilson Room B)
Tuesday	1:30 am	The Leading Edge	(Team Wilson Room A)
	6:00 am	Dust Buster	(Team Wilson Room A)
	6:30 am	The Private Eyes	(Team Wilson Room B)
	8:30 am	Materials Dept.	(Team Wilson Room A)
	2:00 pm	Quality Musketeers	(Team Wilson Room B)
	2:40 pm (2)	Ultra Fitness/Chs Team	(Team Wilson Room A)
	7:30 pm (3)	Second Shift Safety	(Team Wilson Room A)
	10:00 pm	Piece Makers	(Team Wilson Room A)
Wednesday	6:30 am	Master Packers	(Team Wilson Room A)
	6:30 am (4)	Dusk Till Dawners	(Team Wilson Room B)
	8:30 am	Materials Dept.	(Team Wilson Room A)
	10:00 am	Cash Caddies	(Team Wilson Room A)
	10:00 am	Touch of Class	(Team Wilson Room B)
	11:00 am	Mama Narude	(Team Wilson Room A)
	2:00 pm *	The Buffettes	(Team Wilson Room B)
	2:15 pm	Four in One	(Team Wilson Room A)
	3:00 pm	JIT'ers	(Team Wilson Room A)
	3:00 pm	The Transformers	(Team Wilson Room B)
	7:30 pm	Logo Express	(Team Wilson Room A)
	10:00 pm	Buffaroos	(Team Wilson Room B)
	10:30 pm	Midnight Dwellers	(Team Wilson Room A)
	11:00 pm	Quality Check	(Team Wilson Room B)
Thursday	6:30 am (4)	Dusk Till Dawners	(Team Wilson Room A)
	6:30 am	All Nighters	(Team Wilson Room B)
	8:30 am	Materials Dept.	(Team Wilson Room A)
	10:00 am	Scheduling Meeting	(Team Wilson Room A)
	10:30 am	Logomotion	(Team Wilson Room B)
	11:00 am	Accounting Dept.	(Team Wilson Room A)
	2:15 pm	Barwell Trail	(Team Wilson Room A)
	2:30 pm	Injection Section	(Team Wilson Room B)
	7:30 pm	Tampo Maniacs	(Conference Room)
	7:30 pm	World-Class Packers	(Training Complex)
	7:30 pm	Final Touch	(Team Wilson Room A)
	7:30 pm	Top Coaters	(Team Wilson Room B)
	10:30 pm	Midnight Range Riders	(Team Wilson Room A)
Friday	6:00 am	3-Pc Commandos	(Team Wilson Room A)
	8:30 am	Materials Dept.	(Team Wilson Room A)
	2:00 pm	Elite Fleet	(Team Wilson Room A)
	2:00 pm	Sluggers	(Team Wilson Room B)
	6:30 pm *	Second to None	(Team Wilson Room A)

* Denotes changes from last schedule.
(1) Second & fourth week of each month.
(2) Ultra Fitness-first and third week & Chs Team-second and fourth week.
(3) First & third week of each month.
(4) Alternate weeks at 10:00 and 10:30 pm.

Wilson Sporting Goods Company

The Private Eyes team conducted a project in which they examined the size variation of the three-piece golf ball after the molding operation. The team used statistical quality control (SQC) techniques. Team members believed this project could be useful in determining whether the current process was under control and how much size variation should be expected from the process. The study was conducted using histograms and X-bar and R charts. From this study recommendations were made that put the team in position to:

➤ Quickly spot "special" causes of variation,
➤ Know when to adjust sizes,
➤ Know when the process improvements actually worked, and
➤ Reduce overall ball-size variation.

Wilson has six nonmanufacturing functions: materials, production engineering, human resources, quality, research and development, and accounting. The accounting function will be the focus of the remainder of this chapter.

Accounting Support of Total Quality Management Concepts

The accounting department's support for TQM concepts can be explained only as a part of the total corporate culture. This culture is centered around the mission/vision statement described in the introduction and reflects a total commitment by all departments, both manufacturing and support, to TQM concepts.

■ Accounting Department Mission Statement

After the plantwide mission/vision statement shown in Exhibit 5-3 was completed, each department was asked to develop a mission statement consistent with and supportive of the plantwide mission statement. The accounting department created the following mission statement:

> Our mission is to provide relevant, accurate reporting of financial information on a timely basis to plant and corporate associates for use in guiding appropriate managerial decisions.

The Accounting Department [personnel] will perform our professional duties in accordance with applicable laws, regulations, and technical standards. We will exercise a high standard of ethical conduct, integrity, and confidentiality. Our department will maintain an appropriate level of professional competence by on-going development of our knowledge and skills. We will align all activities with the plant's strategic goal of

Exhibit 5-5. Customer Identified by Accounting Area

Accounting Area	Customer
Payroll	1. Hourly associates 2. Salaried coaches
Account payments	1. Vendors/suppliers 2. Engineering 3. Department heads
Receptionist	1. Visitors 2. Anyone receiving mail 3. Anyone sending mail 4. Anyone receiving a phone call 5. Anyone making a phone call
Management accountants/controller	1. Local management 2. Division headquarters 3. Corporate headquarters

becoming a world-class manufacturer, and the departmental goal of providing excellent customer service (Estes 1993).

This mission statement helps identify the goals, objectives, and tasks of the accounting department personnel, but the continuous improvement philosophy drives their actions.

One of the first tasks of the accounting department was to identify its customers; it discovered that most were internal. Exhibit 5-5 describes the accounting area of responsibility and the customer. Consistent with the TQM approach in the mission statement, teams were organized to improve service to both internal and external customers. Accounting personnel have been organized into two teams and various committees. The two teams are the administrative team and the management team.

■ The Administrative Team

The administrative team is composed of five nonexempt associates who are responsible for payroll, accounts payable, telephone communications, and mail. Each team member has been cross-trained to function in all the responsibilities of the team.

This team structure can be compared to a golf team. All members perform the same duties but are measured as individuals, and their combined efforts or scores measure the success of the team.

When the team was first organized, each member had a specifically assigned duty. The team coach wanted to cross-train each member and envisioned that team members would trade duties so each member would become familiar with the duties of the others. When the coach approached the team members, he explained the goal of cross-training all members in all areas of their collective responsibilities and stated,

> ...tell me how you want to do it. Do you want to do it a day at a time, a week at a time, or a month at a time? I want you to be responsible for accounts payable, payroll, the telephone switchboard, and the mail. I want you to think of your department as five persons owning your own business, which is to disburse Wilson's checks to vendors for purchases and associates for payroll. You are also to handle your associates' mail, greet their customers, and route their telephone calls. How would you like to rotate your duties? (Estes 1993)

After reviewing the situation, the team members presented the coach with the suggestion that each member take responsibility for a portion of the accounts payable and a portion of the payroll. Also each member would spend a portion of each day handling the mail, greeting customers, and routing associates' telephone calls on the switchboard. This proposal was an even better plan than the coach's. It would guarantee that all members of the team would be cross-trained in duties, plus it would fix responsibility for each vendor and payroll associate with a specific member of the team.

This method of dividing responsibilities would facilitate any follow-up for unusual situations without having to spend an inordinate amount of time explaining the situation to all members of the team when something unusual occurred. With this new approach, each team member could fill in for another, if necessary, due to illness, vacation, or other reasons.

When the administrative team was first organized, a name was needed to identify them. Because a part of their responsibilities was to reimburse travel expenses, they named themselves the Tightwads. Later they decided that their customers perceived this name negatively and changed it to Figure Watchers. Still later, the team decided that the new name also was perceived negatively and changed it to their current name of Cash Caddies.

An example of how the TQM concepts are used by the Cash Caddies is the development of the APPLE (Accounts Payable Problems Lower Efficiency) report (see Exhibit 5-6). This report gives the number of invoices processed for payment and the number not processed with the reason for not processing them. The unprocessed invoices are listed in a Pareto chart by the reason they could not be processed.

Exhibit 5-6. Accounts Payable Problems Lower Efficiency Report

Types of Problems	92 Jul	92 Aug	92 Sept	92 Oct	92 Nov	92 Dec	93 Jan	93 Feb	93 Mar	93 Apr	93 May	93 Jn	Last 12 mo	(%)
Price difference	16	20	27	27	25	31	42	30	18	16			252	26.3
Multiple packing lists	14	12	17	9	22	5	17	16	5	2			119	12.4
Error on receiver	11	28	2	17	6	13	16	12	4	9			118	12.3
No receiver	2	13	17	9	4	21	14	10	2	5			97	10.1
PO error	6	12	6	11	0	4	7	14	8	6			74	7.7
Other/miscellaneous	3	3	7	10	5	6	19	7	6	7			73	7.6
Item rec'd not on PO	5	8	6	2	6	5	12	5	3	0			52	5.4
No FedEx #	8	4	9	6	3	1	6	7	0	0			44	4.6
Overshipment	7	3	9	4	3	3	9	5	1	4			48	5.0
No packing slip	6	5	2	0	2	1	6	8	9	7			46	4.8
No PO	2	2	5	3	2	1	7	4	7	3			36	3.8
Total invoices that cannot be processed for payments	80	110	107	98	78	91	155	118	63	59	0	0	959	100.0
Total invoices processed	1,074	716	1,232	862	950	761	1,036	1,142	1,315	781	0	0	9,869	
% of invoices with paperwork problems	7.4%	15.4%	8.7%	11.4%	8.2%	12.0%	15.0%	10.3%	4.85%	7.6%	ERR	ERR	9.7%	

Monthly distribution of problems

Types of problems	Jul	Aug	Sept	Oct	Nov	Dec	Jan	Feb	Mar	Apr	May	Jn
Price difference	20.0%	18.2%	25.2%	27.6%	32.1%	34.1%	27.1%	25.4%	28.6%	27.1%	ERR	ERR
Multiple packing list	17.5%	10.9%	15.9%	9.2%	28.2%	5.5%	11.0%	13.6%	7.9%	3.4%	ERR	ERR
Error on receiver	13.8%	25.5%	1.9%	17.3%	7.7%	14.3%	10.3%	10.2%	6.3%	15.3%	ERR	ERR
No receiver	2.5%	11.8%	15.9%	9.2%	5.1%	23.1%	9.0%	8.5%	3.2%	8.5%	ERR	ERR
PO error	7.5%	10.9%	5.6%	11.2%	0.0%	4.4%	4.5%	11.9%	12.7%	10.2%	ERR	ERR
Other/miscellaneous	3.8%	2.7%	6.5%	10.2%	6.4%	6.6%	12.3%	5.9%	9.5%	11.9%	ERR	ERR
Item rec'd not on PO	6.3%	7.3%	5.6%	2.0%	7.7%	5.5%	7.7%	4.2%	4.8%	0.0%	ERR	ERR
No FedEx #	10.0%	3.6%	8.4%	6.1%	3.8%	1.1%	3.9%	5.9%	0.0%	0.0%	ERR	ERR
Overshipment	8.8%	2.7%	8.4%	4.1%	3.8%	3.3%	5.8%	4.2%	1.6%	6.8%	ERR	ERR
No packing slip	7.5%	4.5%	1.9%	0.0%	2.6%	1.1%	3.9%	6.8%	14.3%	11.9%	ERR	ERR
No PO	2.5%	1.8%	4.7%	3.1%	2.6%	1.1%	4.5%	3.4%	11.1%	5.1%	ERR	ERR
	100%	100%	100%	100%	100%	100%	100%	100%	100%	100%		

This report focuses attention on the reason why problems arise in paying invoices and what action can be taken to correct the problem. When the problems are properly identified, members of the Cash Caddies meet with their internal customers and/or the suppliers to correct the problems.

■ The Management Team

The management team is composed of four members and is in the early stages of organization. Each member is assigned a functional area of responsibility, such as the general ledger, fixed asset ledger, product costing, or inventory valuation. While the functional areas are assigned to a specific individual, all team members will be cross-trained so they can perform in any of the functional areas. Also, certain functions require cooperation. For example, team members work jointly on month-end closings, budgets, forecasting, and financial statements.

This team structure is comparable to a volleyball team. Each member has an assigned position but moves to cover other areas of the department as needed.

■ Accounting Department Use of TQM Tools

Training has just begun for both teams to become self-directed work teams (SDWT). This training will be a vehicle for more empowerment, such as having the teams schedule their own vacations and leave time. The TQM measurement tools used by both teams are listed in Exhibit 5-7.

■ Committee Assignments

Members from either of the accounting teams may be assigned to serve on input/output committees. Input committees are organized to meet with providers or suppliers of information to obtain the best possible flow of information between the two departments or entities. Output committees are organized to meet with customers who will provide suggestions for improving services.

■ Accounting Efficiencies of TQM Concepts

It is obvious that the adoption of TQM concepts has made the accounting function more efficient. Because of the reduction in all inventories, the auditors no longer observe the taking of the year-end inventory. From 1986 until 1994, the increase in accounting staff has been only 43%.

Other increases have been other salaried personnel, 105%; hourly personnel, 185%; payroll dollars, 240%; accounts payable, 275%; and production volume, 265% (see Exhibit 5-8).

Management has suggested to corporate headquarters that only quarterly closings be conducted because Wilson's information system is so reliable. There have been no significant differences in financial reports at month-end closings from the data before month-end adjustments.

Implications for the Accounting Function

1. A paradigm shift in attitude is required to maximize the value of accounting services. The attitude that accounting is a separate department with its own agenda and timetable for completing accounting functions must give way to the attitude that time and effort will be contributed to those who use or need information. The usefulness of information that traditionally has been provided needs to be challenged, and the only information provided should be that requested by current decision makers. This change may require reformatting financial data or reporting a different kind of information, such as nonfinancial data that

Exhibit 5-7. Accounting Department Measurement Tools

Tool	Use
Pareto analysis	1. Payroll problems 2. Accounts payable problems
Pareto charts	1. Payroll problems 2. Accounts payable problems
Pie charts	To show a distribution of the above-listed problems
Bar charts	1. To show accuracy of checks 2. To show accuracy of inventories 3. To show safety/housekeeping compliance with standards
Run/control chart	For inventory control
Cause-and-effect (fishbone) diagrams	For problem solving
Flow charting	1. Analyze systems and processes 2. Train new team members 3. Prepare for benchmarking

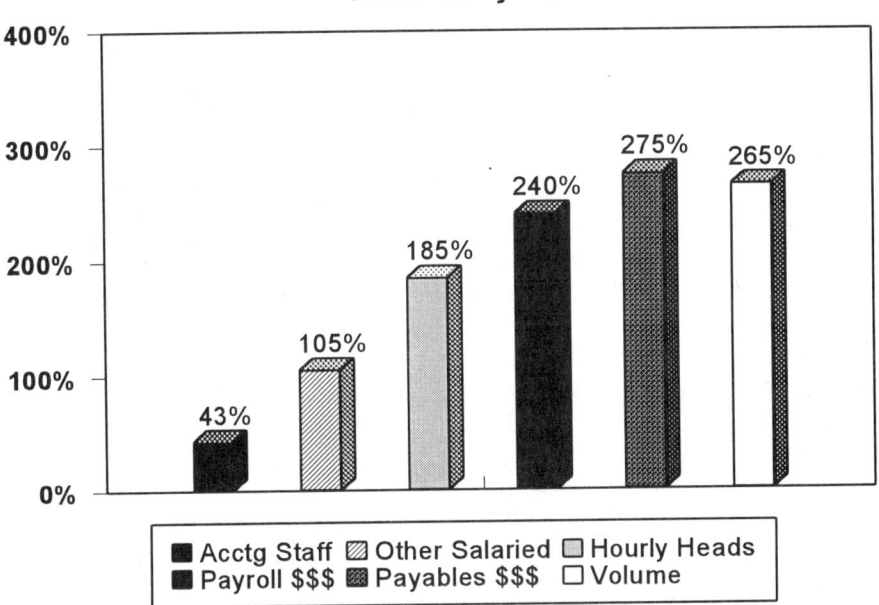

Exhibit 5-8. Plant Growth Comparisons
1986A vs. Fy 94P

- Acctg Staff: 43%
- Other Salaried: 105%
- Hourly Heads: 185%
- Payroll $$$: 240%
- Payables $$$: 275%
- Volume: 265%

can monitor some function or system. It is important to let the customer or information user decide what is needed, with the accounting personnel providing samples of ideas as options from which the customer may choose.

2. *Management accounting personnel must be trained more broadly to understand all the functions of their employer.* The information needed by various segments of a business probably will vary from that traditionally provided. To fulfill internal customers' information needs, accounting personnel must thoroughly understand the functions being performed by the internal customer.

3. *Management accounting personnel must be intimately involved with the design of the information system to assure that internal controls are provided where feasible and that proper information is provided for internal and external customer needs.* Changes in management styles and philosophies have altered the need for various accounting internal controls. For example, the implementation of a just-in-time production system reduces or eliminates the need for several accounting controls over inventory. Careful creative thinking must be employed in the design of the information system to retain only those accounting internal controls necessary while providing downstream information for both internal and external needs. The inter-

nal needs are determined jointly with the internal customer while the external needs for stockholders, creditors, and government entities are determined by the accounting personnel.

4. *Management accounting personnel must be as computer literate as possible.* The computer has become a powerful tool for both producing products and providing information. The efficiencies that can be obtained using the computer are directly associated with the knowledge of how to use it. Fast-breaking and continual developments in the computer environment, both in hardware and software, require constant monitoring. The cost of hardware is falling continually while the hardware is providing more and more capacity. The various software packages that appear on the market almost daily offer better information more quickly than existing software. The accountant must evaluate the new hardware and software to determine if the increase in efficiency can justify their cost.

5. *Management accounting personnel must become economic educators.* As work teams use the principle of empowerment, they must understand the economic impact of their decisions before implementation. For example, if a team would like to replace three parts with one new and more expensive part, they must determine if it is economically feasible to do so. The management accountant can point out the differences in cost of materials, labor, and other resources as well as the possible impact on customer satisfaction and revenue differences. The management accountant is best qualified and in the best position to understand the total downstream revenue and resource utilization impact and must accept the responsibility to educate the work-team members.

Conclusion

Wilson Sporting Goods Co. has become a world-class competitor in the manufacture of golf balls by implementing the TQM philosophies and concepts. These philosophies and concepts have extended to all manufacturing and service departments including the accounting department. In fact, the company culture is so designed and developed that departmental lines are less visible and all employees feel more a part of the total company than merely their department.

References

Estes, J. 1993. Controller, Wilson Sporting Goods Co. On-site interview, May 12-13.

Wilson Sporting Goods Co. 1992. 1993 Shingo Prize — Excellence in Manufacturing — Application.

6

Management Accounting and Manufacturing Quality Commitment

Gates Rubber Company

Introduction

The Gates Corporation is a privately owned international organization consisting of five subsidiaries: the Gates Rubber Company; Gates Energy Products; Gates Formed-Fibre Products, Inc.; Gates Power Drive Products, Inc.; and Gates Land Company. The 81-year-old firm is headquartered in Denver, Colorado.

The Gates Rubber Company is the Gates Corporation's largest subsidiary. It manufactures and markets hose and connector products, V-belts, synchronous belts, conveyor belts, flat belts, and molded rubber products for automotive and industrial customers and boots and carpet underlay. Operations include 16 manufacturing plants in the United States, 20 plants in eight other countries, and three international joint ventures.

Recently, the Gates Rubber Company invested $8 million to turn its Siloam Springs, Arkansas, facility into the most innovative manufacturing plant of its kind in America. The Siloam Springs operation (Gates-Siloam) opened in 1977. It produces automotive V-belts and industrial heavy-duty and light-duty V-belts. Among the markets served are automotive and industrial original equipment manufacturers and replacement part distributors and agricultural, construction, mining, and oil industries. The Gates-Siloam facility is a Gates enriched management (GEM) plant. The GEM system, based on mutual trust and respect among all employees and their ability to work together as a team, is discussed in detail in a later section.

The plant uses cellular manufacturing (sometimes called focused factories) to process products from start to finish within one work area. Each cell is managed by a self-directed team of production employees. These employees continue to take on additional responsibilities and decision-making roles as they become more empowered in the workplace. The traditional supervisor has been replaced by facilitators and team coaches who serve as resources for production and assist self-directed teams in their quest for continuous improvement.

Gates-Siloam has been engaged in many activities aimed at achieving world-class manufacturing status. These activities include total employee involvement, total productive maintenance, total quality control (TQC), just-in-time (JIT) manufacturing, computer-integrated manufacturing, and factory automation. As a result of these new philosophies, Gates-Siloam has earned a variety of awards relating to quality and service. These include the GM SPEAR award, John Deere Certification, Volkswagen Certified Supplier Rating, Class "A" Manufacturing Resource Planning award, and the Ford Q1 award. In 1992, Gates-Siloam was the subject of and host site for an Association for Manufacturing Excellence (AME) conference on "Customer Satisfaction Through Empowered Work Teams," and in 1993 it received the Shingo Prize for Excellence in Manufacturing. In 1994 *Industry Week* considered Gates-Siloam one of the top 25 plants in the United States, and Clemson University awarded Gates-Siloam the 21st Century Organizational Excellence Award.

The receipt of the above-listed awards is supported by the following outcome measures of productivity improvements:

➢ *Total sales.* Total sales increased from $79 million in 1988 to $135 million in 1993.
➢ *Sales per employee.* During the same period, sales per employee rose from around $172,000 to approximately $210,000.
➢ *Standard value output.* The standard value of products manufactured grew from a little over $100,000 per day in 1988 to $230,000 per day in 1993.
➢ *Belt production.* Belt production rose from a little over 20 million in 1988 to 25 million in 1993.
➢ *Manufacturing lead times.* In all cases, manufacturing lead times have dropped from weeks in 1988 to days in 1993. In many cases, belts are started and go to stock during a single shift.
➢ *Increased manufacturing capacity.* Setting up work cells and eliminating inventory have increased production space by 90,000 square feet, a 40% increase in space without any increased investment in brick and mortar.
➢ *Inventory turns.* During the past five years, raw material turns went from seven in 1988 to 17 in 1993, and finished goods turns went from 10 in 1988 to 15 in 1993 (Gates 1993 Shingo Prize Application, p. 34; MacDonald 1993).

Management Support of Total Quality Management Concepts

The TQM culture and organization infrastructure at Gates-Siloam was built on a foundation of three principles: leading, empowering, and partnering.

■ Leading

One of the most important imperatives of leadership is the clear communication of what is expected from one's associates. This expectation is communicated to all Gates-Siloam employees through descriptive statements about Gates vision, Gates quality commitment (GQC), Gates employee recognition process, the GEM system, and Gates new employee orientation.

Gates vision. Gates Rubber Company has taken special care to communicate its mission, values, and vision to all its employees, including those at Gates-Siloam, through a variety of means. These include a Gates-produced video that all employees watch, attendance at GQC classes, new employee orientation meetings, and a placard that each employee receives for easy reference.

Gates quality commitment. Gates-Siloam has made an absolute commitment to quality, and the implementation strategy of the GQC focuses Gates employee actions toward the fulfillment of its mission and vision statements. Each employee receives eight hours of formal class instruction on the GQC strategy.

A part of the quality commitment is the implementation of the Gates quality improvement process (QIP). The QIP model is a systematic approach to improving processes and is flexible enough to use a wide variety of improvement methods, tools, and techniques. A complete QIP manual has been published and is available to all employees, who also receive a quick reference guide to QIP when they attend the QIP class (see Chapter 6 Appendix, page 82).

Gates employee recognition process. As part of the GQC, a three-level recognition process has been installed. The purpose of the recognition is to reflect the feeling that a particular completed action or assignment is important to Gates and is consistent with GQC values. The three levels of recognition are:

➢ Continuous recognition for quality performance,
➢ Recognition for business achievement, and
➢ The Charles C. Gates Award for Excellence.

The Gates enriched management system. The GEM system is a unique alternative to the traditional management system. Gates-Siloam was built and continues to operate today on the GEM philosophy. The heart of this philosophy is the belief that employees are the experts at their jobs. They must be completely involved in many job aspects to do quality work. They are asked to recognize and help solve problems on the job. This approach helps break down barriers between employees and management so that everyone works together as a team to make better products more efficiently. The following list details some of the GEM system characteristics:

- There are no time clocks to punch. Each employee is on the honor system to record his or her hours worked through an electronic time card.
- Lunch and break times are paid.
- There are no distinctions between management and nonmanagement personnel with regard to parking, break rooms, and other such privileges.
- Casual dress is standard, and managers do not wear suits.
- An open-door policy prevails. In fact, there are no doors. Managers are situated in open-bay office areas with other support personnel.

New employee orientation. Every new employee of Gates-Siloam attends a paid one-week orientation seminar when first hired. In this seminar the employee learns about the GEM philosophy, GQC, and employee empowerment. A cross-section of managers, facilitators, support personnel, and production employees participate in the new employee orientation seminar to emphasize that all employees are a part of the Gates-Siloam team.

■ Empowering

The empowering process whereby responsible decisions are made by employees at the production level has required a paradigm shift about supervision, increased education on the part of employees, and team-building efforts by all employees.

Supervision paradigm shift. The empowering concept was introduced by giving decision authority to work cells. Line supervision was eliminated, and the traditional role of the supervisor as overseer, disciplinarian, and fire fighter was phased out. Former supervisory positions have been eliminated, and the supervisors have changed their roles to facilitators, taken other assignments, or left Gates.

Increased employee education. For the work cell employees to accept the role of decision maker, they have to be better educated, informed, and trained. This education is accomplished by outside programs offered by colleges and professional organizations as well as by in-house programs such as short courses on the use of computers.

Gates Rubber Company

Team-building efforts by all employees. The real key to the success of empowerment is the ability of employees to form teams that work together to identify and solve problems that have reduced productivity and quality. Gates-Siloam has a wide variety of formal cross-functional teams. A good example of a successful cross-functional team is the factory support team. Each of the four factories within the plant has a support team comprising scheduling, quality, maintenance, process engineering, belt technical, and training facilitators. These teams meet at least weekly to discuss current issues and to review progress on various projects. Representatives from plant support areas, such as accounting or information systems, frequently are invited to these meetings. As the employees participate on the various teams and gain understanding and confidence, they make better and more informed decisions that are continually improving the quality and productivity at Gates-Siloam.

■ Partnering

Where there are mutual interests between the goals of Gates-Siloam and other parties, it is important to enter into partnership agreements so that all parties understand how their goals may be attained and what is expected from the other parties. Gates-Siloam has developed partnerships with their suppliers, customers, employees, and community.

Partnering with suppliers. In the value chain from raw material to satisfied customer, Gates-Siloam does not control the quality of its raw materials. The suppliers do, however, and it becomes important to secure a stable source of the best-qualified raw materials possible. Gates-Siloam has entered into agreements with its suppliers that permit the evaluation of supplier quality control systems.

Partnering with customers. Customer satisfaction is the next step in the value chain, and Gates-Siloam is constantly evaluating customer relations to make sure their customers are satisfied. A cross-functional team comprising members from manufacturing at Gates-Siloam and corporate representatives from product control, customer service, sales, and marketing make visits to Gates' customers. This team evaluates Gates-Siloam's performance according to the following criteria: on-time performance, order policies, receiving orders, shipping, lead times, samples and new products, return policy, packaging and branding, inspection/certification/testing, labor contracts, vacation shutdowns, communications, and other issues.

Partnering with employees. All actions on the part of employees are the results of partnering; however, one particular area, the safety program, is singled out for review. This is an area of mutual interest to the employees and to Gates-Siloam top management.

To help prevent accidents and provide a safe workplace, Gates-Siloam adopted the DuPont safety training observation program (STOP). STOP is designed to help eliminate injuries through the systematic practice of observing, correcting, preventing, and reporting unsafe acts. All employees attend seven sessions of training that require one hour of classroom participation as well as out-of-class preparation. Top management at Gates-Siloam elected to have all employees take the expanded supervision version of the program, which includes self-study, group discussion, videotapes, and on-the-job applications.

Any act or situation that presents a safety hazard is reported. The report is never used for disciplinary purposes but rather as a method to eliminate such hazards. This practice enhances respect for both employees and Gates-Siloam and fosters the concept of partnering.

Partnering with the community. To be a good citizen in a small community, especially where Gates-Siloam is a large employer of community residents, it is imperative that the company be involved in many community activities. Some activities Gates-Siloam has supported are:

- Recycling activities/Environmental Fair,
- Adopt-a-school program,
- United Way,
- Child development center,
- Scholarship program, and
- Needy children Christmas gift program.

Gates-Siloam is taking a positive approach to being a good citizen by being active in community programs.

In summary, the business culture is built around the TQM philosophy and is being implemented through good leadership, empowerment, and partnering concepts.

Accounting Support of Total Quality Management Concepts

Because of the integrative nature of the TQM philosophy, many accounting department actions were driven by the need to support manufacturing excellence. Probably the most significant contribution was the development of the information system network.

■ The Information System Network

The current information system at Gates-Siloam is the result of an extensive network implementation project. The network has 175 work stations that extend throughout the plant. The work stations, which are 80386 or 80486 machines, are connected to four different file servers using Novell

Netware. This network also is connected to the mainframe computer at the home office in Denver, Colorado. The system has five LaserJet printers situated throughout the plant, a fax modem to fax screens from within various applications, and a chatterbox machine, which enables users to phone in or out by modem. The network provides 24-hours-a-day, seven-days-a-week access to such mission-critical tasks as inventory, order tracking, and maintenance systems. All work station and network users are able to communicate with each other via an e-mail system, and all users have access to word processing, spreadsheet, graphics, desktop publishing, and other software.

A personal appointment calendar allows each user to keep track of his or her appointments and to maintain a running to-do list. If a meeting is required, the pertinent information, such as the time, place, and duration, is entered, and the system will automatically schedule the meeting room, send a message to those invited, identify any conflicts with other meetings, and update the appointment calendars of those invited when they confirm that they will attend.

The payroll and accounts payable payments are processed at corporate headquarters in Denver after Gates-Siloam unloads all pertinent information. Because of the interactive connection between the corporate mainframe and the network, these tasks are much less daunting.

Perhaps the most extensive and widely used system on the network is the manufacturing system referred to as M1. The cost accountant at Gates-Siloam was selected to lead in the design of the M1 system because he had some knowledge of and an interest in computers and materials management and control.

This system is primarily a material-planning and order-tracking system that facilitates on-line schedules, order maintenance, material planning, material ordering and delivery, production reporting, on-line specifications, electronic pick list, backflushing, engineering change request, and capacity planning. The cost accountant is now in charge of the M1 system and another accountant has been hired to work in the cost accounting function.

The manufacturing system also supports a sophisticated process control and monitoring system. Process studies are conducted on-line in real time so that corrective action can be taken immediately. Current studies can be monitored from anywhere on the network, and alarms can be set up to signal a user when a particular process is drifting out of control. All statistical process control (SPC) data are shared across the network, and summary reports or hard copies of SPC charts can be generated on demand. SPC data may be keyed in by the operator on a keyboard, but, in most cases, a button is pushed on a digital or analog measuring device, such as calipers, or a foot pedal is activated. This SPC system provides a wealth of data for use by operators and task teams engaged in problem solving.

The networking system supports the implementation of MRP II, JIT, and the work-cell concept and thus is a primary support to the TQM philosophies.

■ Other Accounting Department Contributions

Other contributions by the accounting department include cross-training for all the accountants and consulting with various members in the work cells about the economic impact of their decisions.

There are approximately 700 employees but only four accountants — the controller, the cost accountant, and two assistant accountants. The controller is responsible primarily for the general ledger and financial reports; the cost accountant is responsible primarily for product costing; and the two assistant accountants are responsible for accounts payable and payroll. All four accountants have been cross-trained so that each one can complete any of the accounting functions. When one function is behind schedule, any or all of the accountants can work together to get caught up.

The accountants also serve as consultants to various members in the work cells when economic decisions must be made. For example, the work cell may be having difficulty working with a particular raw material and may wish to switch to another product or vendor. Before taking any action, members of the work cell will consult with the cost accountant to determine the total impact on the cost of the product.

Impressions of Accounting Department Contributions to TQM

A good insight into how the accounting department has contributed to the implementation of TQM philosophies and how it may be able to contribute in the future is revealed by the impressions of top management.

■ The First Question

The following responses were given when management was asked, "What role has the management accounting function played in the evolution of your organization toward world-class manufacturing?":

Response of the plant manager:

> It's tough to break away from the traditional cost accounting system — tracking of labor by job codes, elimination of direct labor — and [take] a new look at in-process inventory. Dependency on operator information was a difficult transition for our accounting department (Hoefs 1993).

Response of the operations manager:

As the Siloam Springs plant emerged from the traditional in-line, mass-production manufacturing system to a cellular, just-in-time pull system, the accounting process underwent some changes also. The traditional machine rates were replaced [with] crew rates to reflect the cellular environment. The changing manufacturing concept was timed to correspond with a massive ramp up in the Siloam Springs capacity and output. . . . The costs for 1993 have shown positive variances as the cultural change has taken place and adequate training levels have been reached by teams and individuals. Cost standards will be adjusted in 1994 to show the improvements that have been accomplished (McGarrah 1993).

Response of the materials manager:

Accounting played an important role in providing justification for cellular manufacturing and in determining the optimum team size for each cell. With the conversion to cellular manufacturing, the accounting function revised its cost standards. For the most part, labor standards were simplified to reflect a "team" orientation. Rather than have a labor standard for each operation, an aggregate labor standard is assigned to products to encompass all operations in the cell (McGill 1993).

Response of the controller:

With the factory conversion from an in-line "push" environment to a cellular "pull" environment, one-man, one-machine standard-rate structures had to be revised to reflect cell-crew objectives in accordance with cell-product mix and cell-cure capacities. Overstaffing of cells initially, due to lack of cross-training, created standard cost increases which were difficult to explain to marketing personnel. Since Gates uses product standard costs to measure manufacturing performance, as well as marketing performance, a great deal of corporate skepticism has been expressed regarding cellular manufacturing and empowered work teams. With more adequate cross-training in place, the plant is now beginning to show more effective utilization of manpower; and, beginning in 1994, these improvements will be passed back to marketing in the form of reduced product standard costs (MacDonald 1993).

■ The Second Question

Management was asked a second question: "What role has management accounting played in the implementation of modern manufacturing techniques and management approaches?" The following responses were received:

Response of the plant manager:

Once the new approach was clearly identified and the accounting department could recognize the ease in using the new reporting system—buy-in occurred (Hoefs 1993).

Response of the operations manager:

Accounting has kept the Siloam Springs team up-to-date on standard cost measurements, inventory reductions, and developed cost of quality measurements (McGarrah 1993).

Response of the materials manager:

The accounting function is represented on our Manufacturing Excellence team. This group coordinates and communicates on-going world-class manufacturing processes in our plant. The accounting representative on this team heads up a task team charged with benchmarking our facility against best-in-class for a variety of performance measures.

The accounting function has been involved in developing new information systems to support cell-performance measurement. Each cell constitutes a cost center to which charges for material, supplies, and labor can be allocated. This information is made available on-line and real-time to production via the LAN. The accounting function also identifies other performance measures for use by cell teams to measure and improve daily performance. Cell teams can access information on cure cycles, on-time performance, production, and defect percentages (McGill 1993).

Response of the controller:

[I] and [the cost accountant] have attended seminars regarding ABC costing and, at this point, are not convinced that ABC offers any improvement over what we now have—just a different approach to assigning burden costs to manufacturing activities. We have not taken as active a role as we should in implementing JIT principles, other than tracking progress in inventory reduction. We need to actively pursue the use of TQM concepts to improve our customer service of financial information (MacDonald 1993).

■ The Third Question

The following responses were received from top management when asked, "What changes have you noted in your management accounting function as a result of changes in your manufacturing environment?:

Response of the plant manager:

As teams become empowered and hungry for more information, the accounting department spends time in training operators to make better decisions. More challenges are occurring for operators and managers (Hoefs 1993).

Gates Rubber Company

Response of the operations manager:

The standard cost structure now reflects crew rates in place of the traditional machine standards. The on-line computer network has changed the basic accounting process and has made information more available (McGarrah 1993).

Response of the materials manager:

Due to our network information system, accounting information and other performance measurements are more readily available to employees than ever before. Accounting plays an important role in helping operators to understand, analyze, and act upon this wealth of data. They accomplish this through classes, attendance at cell and factory meetings, and reports developed for specific-task teams (McGill 1993).

Response of the controller:

We are able to do so much more with less manpower due to the development of our PC-based computer network. Information is available so much quicker from the factory floor; consequently, we are able to report progress on factory performance in a more timely manner.

Changing our standard cost structure from individual machine rates to cellular group rates has required major brain surgery on many corporate accounting and industrial engineering people entrenched in Gates' traditional product-costing methods. We are now beginning to prepare them for future brain surgery when we suggest that labor and related fringe costs should perhaps be absorbed as fixed costs rather than variable (MacDonald 1993).

■ The Fourth Question

When top management was asked, "What changes ought to be made in the way management accounting performs its functions to support future information needs of the organization?" the following responses were given:

Response of the plant manager:

The needs and changes forthcoming are so dynamic that it is difficult to predict. I do believe that an in-depth review with problem-solving resolution should be directed at cost-of-quality programs. I believe the accounting department should accept the role of analyzing the quality data and make recommendations to manufacturing as well as to the end customer (Hoefs 1993).

Response of the operations manager:

Accounting needs to take a more proactive approach in moving the accounting process through the continuous-improvement concept. More involvement in the manufacturing process by the accounting group would be helpful. More cost training could be made available by accounting for the Siloam Springs support team (McGarrah 1993).

Response of the materials manager:

Accounting should always strive to be prescriptive rather than just descriptive. Accountants can lend their expertise in plant economics to the many activities that occur within our four walls and become a powerful resource in identifying potential problems and in providing solutions proactively (McGill 1993).

Response of the controller:

We need to direct more effort toward reporting economic impacts before occurrence rather than just being scorekeepers after the fact (MacDonald 1993).

Implications for the Accounting Function

1. Management accountants must be completely involved in the strategic plan of the business. Management accountants must be completely aware of the strategic plan so they can design the information system that will support the plan. Because management must control the critical parts of the strategic plan and the information reported attracts management's attention, the information system must provide the appropriate information. Whether controlling day-to-day operations or making decisions about capital equipment acquisitions, management must be aware of current, accurate, and appropriate information.

2. Management accountants must be knowledgeable and keep current about computer hardware and software. Modern management philosophies demand current information that can be provided only by the latest computer technology. If management accountants are to add value, they must provide this current information at an acceptable cost.

3. Management accountants must understand the economic impacts of all business decisions and be good communicators. When work-cell employees are faced with decisions that have economic implications, they need and want input from someone knowledgeable about economics. Management accountants are the best trained and in the most-informed positions to provide this knowledge and advice. Management at Gates-Siloam has relied on management accountants to communicate to these empowered workers the likely economic results of their actions. Management would like the accountants to be even more proactive in this matter.

4. Management accountants need to accept a stronger role in decision making. In place of simply providing information to others to make decisions, management accountants need to interpret the information they generate and advocate a specific decision or range of decisions that will make the company more profitable. By accepting responsibility for their recommendations, they become more proactive and add more value.

5. *Management accountants must be knowledgeable about all functions of the company from manufacturing to marketing and distribution.* Management accountants are expected to add value by advising all segments of a business about the economic impacts of a decision before it is made. This role will require a forward perspective with a much broader range of knowledge than previously required. They must understand the complete cost structure of manufacturing, marketing, and distribution as well as potential impacts of manufacturing, marketing, and distribution decisions on revenue production.

6. *Management accountants must understand current trends in cost accounting and management methods.* To provide the best economic impact advice and decisions, management accountants must keep abreast of the latest methods of organizing accounting information, such as activity-based management. These methods can help the accountants understand and communicate cost behaviors and economic impacts to others.

Conclusion

The Gates Rubber Company plant at Siloam Springs, Arkansas, has combined one of the most modern information-systems networks and the TQM philosophy into a fully integrated manufacturing plant. The management accountants have been instrumental in this integration and are considered to add value, especially as they advise the empowered workers about the economic impacts of the workers' decisions.

References

Gates Rubber Company, Siloam Springs Division. 1992. 1993 Shingo Prize Application.

Hoefs, B. 1993. Plant manager, Gates Rubber Co., Siloam Springs Division. On-site interview, May 14-15.

MacDonald, J. 1993. Plant controller, Gates Rubber Co., Siloam Springs Division. On-site interview, May 14-15.

McGarrah, L. 1993. Operations manager, Gates Rubber Co., Siloam Springs Division. On-site interview, May 14-15.

McGill, J. 1993. Materials manager, Gates Rubber Co., Siloam Springs Division. On-site interview, May 14-15.

Chapter 6 Appendix

Gates Quality Improvement Process

Everyone in every function involved, empowered, and committed to continuous quality improvement using systematic approaches and processes

Commitment

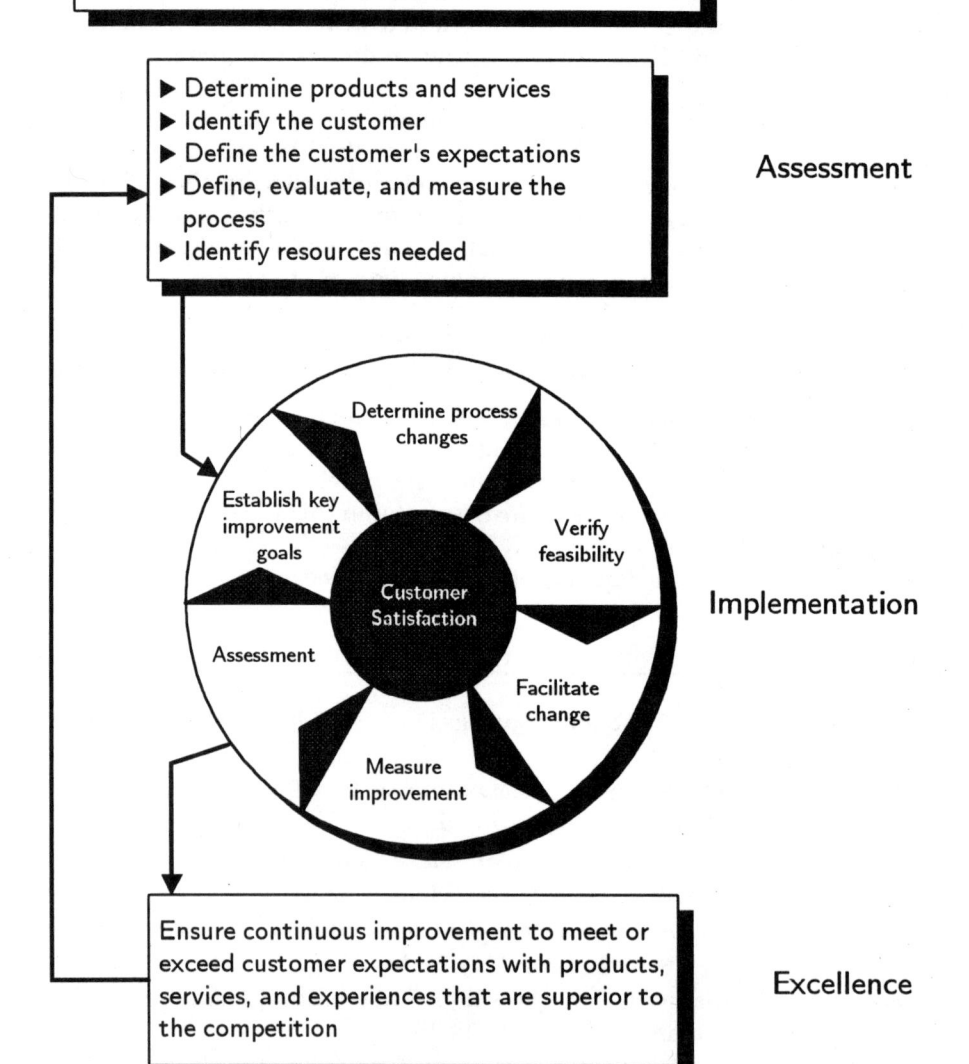

- Determine products and services
- Identify the customer
- Define the customer's expectations
- Define, evaluate, and measure the process
- Identify resources needed

Assessment

Determine process changes
Verify feasibility
Facilitate change
Measure improvement
Assessment
Establish key improvement goals

Customer Satisfaction

Implementation

Ensure continuous improvement to meet or exceed customer expectations with products, services, and experiences that are superior to the competition

Excellence

Gates Rubber Company

QIP Assessment			
QIP Assessment	**Objectives**	**Tasks**	**Tools**
Determine products and services Bar chart	-Clearly describe outputs (products/services) produced by a specific process -Determine process and subprocess boundaries as a basis to identify process improvement opportunities	List process outputs -Individual -Departmental -Company Group as appropriate -Application -Market State objective for the QIP -Creat -Change -Improve	-Action plan -Bar chart -Brainstorming -Pie chart -Product and service grid -Sun diagram
Identify the customer Value chain	-Specifically identify all customers of a process (internal/external) within the customer value chain -Define partnerships required	-List all customers (i.e., recipients of process outputs) -Group customers as appropriate	-Action plan -Block diagram -Brainstorming -Customer value chain -Flow chart -Interview -Product and service grid -Sun diagram
Define the customer's expectations Customer requirements grid	-Analyze current and anticipated future customer needs and expectations -Identify key indicators or standards by which customers measure quality of a product or service -Determine what different customers have in common -Rank customer expectations	-Develop action plan to obtain information -Conduct customer needs analysis -Benchmark as appropriate -Determine customer needs and expectations and confirm mutual understanding	-Action plan -Bar chart -Benchmarking -Brainstorming -Customer needs analysis -Customer requirements grid -Interview -Pie chart -Sampling -Survey -Tree diagram
Define the process Block diagram	-Document process work flows from a high-level perspective -Link process outputs with internal and external customers -Establish process boundaries -Clearly understand how process and subprocesses interconnect across work groups	-Define process boundaries and major groups -Identify process outputs and customers -Identify process inputs and suppliers -Identify subprocesses and work flows -Validate the process definition	-Action plan -Block diagram/process map -Customer value chain -Flow chart -Interview

QIP Assessment			
QIP Assessment	Objectives	Tasks	Tools
Measure the process Trend chart	-Obtain objective data to evaluate quality of products and services -Determine capability of process to satisfy customer -Obtain early identification of potential problems -Determine quality of input from suppliers	-Translate customer needs and expectations into your specifications -Identify pulse points -Determine measurement capability -Brainstorm potential measures and rank -Review and validate existing measures against requirements and key indicators of customer satisfaction -Install new measures as appropriate -Establish reporting and satisfaction feedback system	-Action plan -Bar chart -Brainstorming -Check or tally sheet -Interview -Line or trend chart -Multivoting -Pie chart -Sampling -Survey
Evaluate the process Control chart	-Determine how well the process is meeting or exceeding customer needs and expectations -Identify gaps between process capability and customer satisfaction -Determine cause and impact of process problems -Identify root causes -Provide information to help prioritize key improvement goals	-Collect and review measurement data on process outputs -Construct control charts of data to identify and measure process variability -Compare performance of the process to requirements -Identify root causes -Rank improvement opportunities	-Action plan -Benchmarking -Brainstorming -Cause and effect diagram (fishbone) -Control chart -Decision matrix -Flow chart -Histogram -Interview -Multivoting -Pareto chart -Survey
Identify resources needed Action plan	-Ensure resources are effectively utilized for quality improvements -Determine if existing resources are adequate -Maximize existing resources before new resources are used -Ensure process owners are involved and committed -Identify who can help you close the "gaps" you identified in your process	-Identify resources needed -Plan resource utilization -Involve key stakeholders -Establish and maintain communication and feedback -Identify who will have to approve manpower, materials, or money -List who will actually supply the needed resources	-Action plan

Gates Rubber Company

QIP Implementation

QIP Implementation	Objectives	Tasks	Tools
Establish key improvement goals Pareto chart	-Use information from assessment phase to prioritize key improvement goals -Select vital root causes (those having the greatest impact) -Provide direction for planning/implementing process improvement -Focus on customer needs and expectations -Provide specific, timebound, achievable milestones for improvement	-Review improvement opportunities -Focus on the functional details of the process to determine how it can be improved -List improvement goals -Establish priority of each goal -Select improvement projects	-Action plan -Decision matrix -Flow chart -Histogram -Multivoting -Pareto chart
Determine process change Cause and effect	-Identify high priority options to bring about improvement -Develop the work steps within the action plan necessary to implement the process changes -Identify resources needed to implement the plan	-Select vital changes (those having the greatest impact on the process) -Develop potential solutions -List the steps that must be done. Create a who, what, when, where, how, for each work step within the action plan -Determine new measures as appropriate	-Action plan -Brainstorming -Cause and effect diagram (fishbone) -Decision matrix -Force field analysis -Multivoting -Pareto chart
Verify feasibility Row chart	-Assess capability of planned changes(s) to meet or exceed customer needs and expectations -Assess capability of plan to meet key improvement goals -Determine what could go wrong, assure that your action plan steps address these possibilities -Confirm change has support of key stake-holders and process owners	-Measure and document planned process changes -Determine probability of success -Make changes or additions to your action plan as needed -Obtain resources needed -Confirm change will meet expectations -Problem solve as necessary	-Action plan -Block diagram -Brainstorming -Flow chart -Measurement tools as appropriate -Multivoting

QIP Implementation

QIP Implementation	Objectives	Tasks	Tools
Facilitate change	-Implement action plan -Communicate and work with customers and suppliers affected by change and obtain feedback -Develop teamwork and ownership	-Roll out the plan -Install new measures -Monitor change -Communicate and coordinate with key stakeholders and process partners -Locate new resources and problem solve as needed -Reinforce commitment and support -Acknowledge interim progress	-Action plan

Measure improvement
 	
Histogram
	-Monitor performance of process improvement
	-Collect and communicate on-going customer feedback on process improvement
	-Verify process is performing as planned or make corrections to achieve desired performance
		-Check if measures are still appropriate
		-Monitor process improvements
		-Compare to:
		  -baseline measures
		  -benchmarks
		  -improvement goals
		-Determine if process is performing as planned
		-Collect customer feedback
		-Communicate customer feedback
			-Action plan
			-Bar chart
			-Benchmarking
			-Check sheets
			-Control charts
			-Histogram
			-Interview
			-Line or trend charts
			-Pareto chart
			-Pie chart
			-Sampling
			-Survey

Assess results Trend chart	-Evaluate results of process improvement against key improvement goals, baseline measures, and benchmarks -Determine if additional change is required to meet or exceed customer needs and expectations -Determine if QIP and action plans were followed -Evaluate use of resources for improvement process	-If results do satisfy process improvement, develop an action plan to standardize the process improvement and celebrate -If results do not satisfy process improvement goals, return to assessment -Analyze performance in making process improvement against baseline and other measures -Plan further actions -Perform periodic process review -Provide appropriate feedback and reinforcement	-Action plan -Bar chart -Benchmarking -Check sheets -Control charts -Histogram -Interview -Line or trend charts -Pareto chart -Pie chart -Sampling -Survey

7

Measuring, Communicating, and Educating Management Accounting Challenges at Glacier Vandervell, Inc.

Introduction

Glacier Vandervell, Inc. (GV), formerly JPI Transportation Products, Inc., manufactures heavy-duty engine bearings in its Atlantic, Iowa, production facility. JPI was purchased in 1990 by T&N PLC of Great Britain. This merger has positioned Glacier Vandervell as one of the world's leading producers of engine bearings.

Much of the success at GV has been attributed to its Real Participative Management (RPM) program, a total employee involvement/participative management concept adopted in 1989. The operational achievements of GV have included:

➤ 58% reduction in scrap,
➤ Reduction in cost of quality from 14.9% to 6.8%,
➤ 73% reduction in total inventory,
➤ 40% reduction in annual rework dollars,
➤ 92% reduction in customer returns,
➤ 13% increase in first pass acceptance,
➤ 99.6% customer service levels.

In 1991 Glacier Vandervell was awarded the Shingo Prize for Excellence in American Manufacturing.

The Glacier Vandervell Production Environment

As is typical across the Shingo manufacturing culture, the company relies heavily on employee participation. Thomas Anderson, operations manager and former controller, defines participation as "giving people a voice in their area of expertise." RPM calls for the formation of action teams that include members from both production and service functions within the plant (maintenance, quality control, production, engineering, and accounting). These teams are formed to solve problems that are routinely identified from continuous improvement activities (Shaw 1993).

The GV plant floor is organized into cellular just-in-time (JIT) production lines (sometimes referred to as focused factories) for each family of products. Bottleneck operations are being managed by pacing JIT line capacity by the slowest machine in that line. The movement to cellular manufacturing has significant implications for management accounting and will be discussed in more detail in a later section.

GV has been actively promoting lean manufacturing techniques used successfully by innovative Japanese manufacturers. For example, it has been actively employing setup reduction techniques such as single-minute exchange of die (SMED). Some setups have decreased from 16 hours to two hours as a result of employee action teams. The plant goal is someday to have 10-minute setups (Shaw 1993).

The Shingo culture also calls for partnering activities with suppliers. Partnering encourages better cooperation between the manufacturer and vendor to improve materials quality and on-time delivery performance. A GV action team traveled to a supplier in Caldwell, Ohio, to resolve a scrap problem with steel coil, the major raw material in the production of engine bearings. The method used by the supplier to cut the coil was causing alloy to chip off and become embedded in the bearings, resulting in excessive scrap. Through the combined efforts of the GV action team and the supplier, the cutting approach was altered to resolve the scrap problem (Shaw 1993).

The synchronization of supplier deliveries to coincide with the GV JIT philosophy remains a challenging problem, despite the fact that the major raw material (steel coil) comes from an affiliated company. Controller Duane Russell (1993) explains, "One of the problems we have in manufacturing is that we turn inventory 18-20 times per year, which is pretty good for a manufacturer. However, our suppliers who supply us the coil stock are on a four- to six-week cycle. We incur problems because the GV cycle is two to three weeks."

As a result, raw materials inventory is often higher than the GV lead times require. Despite somewhat limited control over coil stock inventory, GV was still able to pursue other waste-reduction strategies: "We felt that if we could focus our time on reducing waste of materials, time, and overhead, that would be the best way to achieve quality and add value to the product," said Russell.

The Impact of Cellular Manufacturing

In the past, an auto bearing might be routed in batch mode through multiple specialized machining centers located throughout the plant. Because these machining centers served all product lines, it was necessary to change dies every time a different product line was run. Because of the relative transport distances between machining centers and the time spent in the setup/changeover process, large batch sizes were run to maximize the efficiencies on individual machines. Thus, the batch mode contributed significantly to the problem of excess inventories.

The cellular manufacturing approach is a significant departure from the batch manufacturing mode. With the cellular approach, equipment for a family of products is configured together within a production cell. These cells are designed with the flexibility to handle small batch sizes. Furthermore, the pace of the cell is set to the capacity of the slowest machine or bottleneck. In other words, faster machines are not allowed to produce excess inventory just for the purpose of maintaining high utilization rates. The flow of products through each cell is therefore "pulled" by customer demand, restricted only by existing capacities.

■ Cellular Manufacturing and Quality

Quality also improves in a cellular configuration because all operations for a given product or product family are performed sequentially within the cell. Defects in a previous operation should be noted immediately before significant scrap is generated. However, in a batch manufacturing mode, an entire defective batch might be generated before the defect is detected at the next station (Knop 1993).

■ Cellular Manufacturing Impact on Management Accounting

Production Manager Clark Knop notes that a key accounting change precipitated by modern manufacturing techniques has been due to the change from a batch manufacturing mode to continuous flow cellular manufacturing. Because the pace at which each piece proceeds through the operations within the cell is governed by the speed of the slowest machine, faster machines have been slowed down to minimize inventory buildup in front of the slower bottleneck operations. This practice initially distorted output from the standard cost system by showing that pieces were increasing in cost because of lower utilization rates. This result appeared to contradict the expectation that savings would result by changing to a continuous flow cellular environment. Furthermore, the accounting system was failing to capture the improved throughput, lower inventory levels, and improved quality made possible by the switch to the cellular environment. Human Resources Manager Kurt Wanninger notes that as a result, the standards within the accounting system had to be adapted to reflect the bottleneck rate.

Anderson believes that the concept of cellular manufacturing has destroyed traditional cost accounting. Because the cellular approach is output oriented rather than cost oriented, the same rules do not apply anymore. Where measurements used to be focused on each individual machine, they are now based on the bottleneck throughput (Anderson 1993).

Management Accounting Challenges at Glacier Vandervell

Among the management accounting challenges at GV are developing meaningful performance measures, communicating performance results effectively, and educating the workforce about the financial consequences of their actions.

■ Toward Meaningful Accounting Measurements

When a manufacturing cell comes up with ideas that help improve throughput, reduce costs, or increase quality, it likes to have measures that provide evidence of that improvement. At present, these measurements are made primarily at the manufacturing level, particularly because the measurements are done in units rather than dollars. Russell would like to be able to take this one step further by being able to show how this improvement added to the bottom line.

Plant productivity is measured by sales dollars per employee hour. Direct and indirect hours are included in the measurement of hours. One strength of this measure is that it includes all labor; the measure cannot be manipulated to exclude employees not directly involved in manufacturing. However, the measure is not very useful from a decision-making standpoint (Knop 1993).

Knop relates that one labor productivity measure used on the line is the number of hours earned, which is a measure of actual run hours (not including downtime or meeting time). This measure is financially driven and eventually is converted to dollars. According to Knop, a weakness of this measure is that it is not very meaningful to workers on the line. He believes that workers would prefer a measure such as the number of pieces produced. In other words, workers manufacture bearings; they are not manufacturing earned hours.

Knop believes that variance analysis has little informational or motivational value for the typical line worker. He believes that measures should reflect what the workers do—that is, they make bearings. Therefore the system should tell these workers, "This is how many bearings you should have made today . . . or this is how many bearings you made."

Knop believes that eventually the system must be able to communicate the dollar impact of manufacturing throughput in terms of sales and costs in a manner that is meaningful to line workers. Presently, the focus is on the number of pieces produced. While GV hopes to make the work cells self-directed, Wanninger feels that until meaningful measures of performance are developed, cell workers will not have this capability.

■ Accounting Literacy for the Production Employee

In developing appropriate measures of the financial impact of manufacturing operations, accountants must consider the production employee's level of financial sophistication. Clearly, financial measures will have little motivational value if they are not understood by the workers.

> Education of employees is critical if financial measures are to be meaningful. They need to understand some of the basic terms of financial performance. It is a fact of life that companies are financially driven. Companies obviously have to be profitable. Accounting has an important role in educating the employees to increase their understanding of financial measures. It's very difficult to explain to a person working out on a line whether a part is profitable. You start talking about direct costs, indirect costs, fixed costs, variable costs . . . It's all based on volume. If you start talking about that type of thing to people who don't have an accounting background, you just confuse them (Knop 1993).

The restricted financial background of production employees may limit the benefits of modern accounting developments. For example, Russell believes that ABC can be vital in an environment such as GV's where commitments to suppliers can run several years into the future. In his opinion, ABC would provide a truer picture of the cost structure before such a commitment is entered into. However, one of the difficulties associated with implementing systems such as ABC is the level of understanding cell employees have about such concepts as overhead and cash flow. He relates, "Many people in the plant did not understand the difference between incurring expenses on the income statement and committing the dollars on a purchase order. Education must take place out on the line so that people who are authorized to incur expenses understand what GV is trying to accomplish."

Russell believes that the GV plant probably performs more "management accounting" than most other plants because the workforce has not been trained to develop and track their own measures. "When people learn how to correlate activity in the cell to the achievement of plant goals then we [management accounting] will be freed up for more proactive pursuits."

He emphasizes that in accounting, more time must be spent on education [of the workforce] and less time on busy work. He sees several opportunities to eliminate nonvalue-added activities such as excess paperwork and manual processes that can be automated. "If the customer knew they paid a penny per bearing for some of the extra things we do, they wouldn't want to pay that penny. In my mind that's what value-added boils down to." He notes that a training process is underway to prepare line workers to assume more of the measurement responsibility.

■ Improving Accounting Communications

Anderson believes that more information from accounting can give workers the information they need to improve waste management. If workers know that a particular bearing sells for $37 they may take special precautions in the handling of that product. Even in the case of less expensive bearings, the worker should know that every scrapped bearing is a loss of perhaps $1. Anderson asks, "If they [the workers] are not educated in what these parts cost, how can they make decisions?"

Anderson has observed a pronounced change toward more openness with employees. The movement has been from a position of total secrecy to a full disclosure of information. Formerly, product selling prices were guarded as trade secrets. "Plant accountants did not even know [the prices]. . . . Now, we tell employees, 'this sells for _____.'" Anderson also has seen an evolution in accounting communications from "What do you want to know?" to "We *want* you to know." For example, the financial statements now are posted for employees. Anderson emphasizes that "for participative management to succeed, there cannot be secrets. . . . We want them to question. . . . Who spent money on travel and entertainment? . . . What is going on in the marketplace? . . . How does that affect me?"

■ More Consulting. . .Less Gatekeeping

Anderson sees an evolution in the role of the management accountant from that of gatekeeper to adviser, from a strictly historical perspective to a future-oriented perspective. Russell adds that "our goal is to provide accurate information on a timely basis and to make sure the information we provide is relevant. . . . When you are running JIT, it is very important that managers not have to thumb through 300 pages of reports every day to try to get the information they need."

Russell believes that the management accounting philosophy should be to train workers to access the information they think they need to run their work cells properly. This attitude contrasts with the old philosophy of "Here is the information we think you need to run the work cell." Once people start to analyze their own information, they see immediately that when garbage is put in the front end, garbage will result from the back end.

Information systems technology has facilitated the consultancy role of management accounting at GV. Programmer Analyst Max Turner notes that many of the later versions of accounting and manufacturing software are being bundled with database querying tools that enable the user to perform ad hoc queries of the system and thus allow for capabilities beyond the programmed reports. He relates that he was able to use the extended query language to give production information about supplies used in the manufacturing process, broken down by supplies on order, supplies received but not paid for, and disbursements for supplies. He adds that the present GV system has an English-language-based query facility that would allow workers on the floor to access the company database interactively.

Queries can be constructed by Turner and stored as menu selections for future use by production workers on the floor. However, GV has made a policy decision to encourage the production floor to use the system capabilities as far as possible, rather than build parallel applications from the query facility to suit individual tastes. Therefore, training and access to the query facility has been restricted to a few persons who management feels can make effective use of this feature. Even then, its use is warranted only when the application system does not already provide a necessary feature (Turner 1993).

Turner relates that it has been only in recent years that manufacturing workers have recognized the benefits of computerization. Before, they were wary of the technology and used it only when absolutely necessary. That attitude has changed in that ideas for new applications are now coming from the floor. Turner believes that employee participation in the development process is very consistent with the RPM philosophy that presently guides the plant. As a result, Turner spends a lot of time on the production floor getting input from production workers.

■ Operational Support at Glacier Vandervell

Russell notes that in competitive industries such as bearings, the focus of management accounting has to be improved competitiveness, cost containment, and productivity improvement. As an example, Russell emphasizes that GV must be very careful to assess the level of volume when quoting price on a part. If a part is quoted based on the assumption it will be run on a high-volume line and then actually is run on a medium-volume line because of capacity constraints, GV may lose money on that order.

Accounting Supervisor Bruce Ohms (1993) notes that accounting sometimes is asked to reevaluate the costing associated with a particular product in the case of specific market quotations. This is to ensure that they are in line with current market conditions or to see if there is any room for pricing adjustments for a special order. For example, if a customer is willing to commit to a higher volume on a particular part, GV may recost the part based on the higher value assumptions.

GV is looking to activity-based costing to support decisions pertaining to the replacement of existing product lines. Ohms points out that with present space limitations, activity-based costing would be useful in determining if an existing line should be replaced with a more profitable line or perhaps a more automated line (Ohms 1993).

In the area of quality, accounting is most involved in tracking scrap levels and inspection costs and reporting this information directly to management as the *cost of quality*.

This measure has four components:

➢ The costs associated with the internal failure of the product (scrap, rework);
➢ The costs of external failure (loss of customer satisfaction, repair, and replacement);
➢ The costs of appraisal (quality monitoring and inspection);
➢ The costs of employee training.

Implications for Management Accounting

1. *Accountants should recognize the level of accounting sophistication of their constituents and be proactive in raising that level.* To ensure that accounting communications have their desired impact, it is clear that accountants must consider their audience. Assumptions that employees understand the basic financial measures may be unwarranted. While it is clear that employees need measures relevant to controlling their immediate operations, they also need to be aware of how their actions affect the well-being of the organization. Without this awareness, even the most sophisticated accounting analyses and reporting cannot be used effectively. Therefore, an important function of management accounting is to educate workers about basic financial measures.

2. *Accountants must be careful that accounting systems recognize the changes wrought by techniques such as cellular manufacturing and continuous flow production.* Management accountants must be alert to changes in manufac-

turing practices that may invalidate traditional efficiency and productivity measures. Accountants must adjust to emerging manufacturing practices involving utilization, excess capacities, and labor efficiencies. With Japanese philosophies such as those adopted by the Shingo Prize recipients, people and machines are not expected to be building products all the time. Employees not actively assembling products can spend time improving processes, improving their skills, and performing productive maintenance on idle equipment. Accounting measurements should not punish these types of activities or provide incentives to engage in overproduction. On the other hand, new accounting measures must be sensitive to the improvements in manufacturing processes. These measures must provide confirmation that workers are indeed doing a good job and that agile manufacturing practices are contributing to bottom-line financial performance.

3. *Accounting can facilitate open financial communications that lead to better operational decisions.* GV has taken the position that open sharing of financial data with employees should provide the opportunity for better decisions. Better understanding by employees of product pricing should provide incentives to prevent scrap and rework. Employees who are informed about the company's relative performance in the marketplace would appear to be easier to motivate. However, employees who are not kept informed of company financial performance may assume the company is more profitable than it really is. Accounting can facilitate communication by developing financial measures that are both sensitive to operational activities and meaningful to production workers.

4. *Accountants should reduce their gatekeeping role and move to a consultancy role.* Just as cellular manufacturing has empowered production workers to implement their own continuous improvements, accountants can empower workers to gather and analyze their own operational data and help them assess the financial impact of their operations. To accomplish this, accountants must change their orientation from that of solely keeping score to providing consultation on how employees can design their own measurement systems and collect or access the data they need in the cell. As production cells accept ownership and responsibility for their own measurements, the quality of data throughout the organization should improve.

Conclusion

GV has demonstrated that accounting systems must be careful not to obscure the benefits of modern manufacturing techniques by focusing on traditional machine utilization and labor efficiency. Accounting systems should never penalize production workers for normal excess capacity that can be used for additional training, process improvement, and productive maintenance.

It is clear that workers must understand the financial impact of their operational activities. The accounting function can facilitate this understanding by assisting the production cells in developing measures that link operational measures to financial impacts. Also, accountants perform a key role in educating workers about financial indicators.

References

Anderson, T. 1993. Operations manager, Glacier Vandervell, Inc. On-site interview, May 5-6.

Knop, C. 1993. Production manager, Glacier Vandervell, Inc. On-site interview, May 5-6.

Ohms, B. 1993. Accounting supervisor, Glacier Vandervell, Inc. On-site interview, May 5-6.

Russell, D. 1993. Controller, Glacier Vandervell, Inc. On-site interview, May 5-6.

Shaw, S. 1993. Line leader, Glacier Vandervell, Inc. On-site interview, May 5-6.

Turner, M. 1993. Programmer/analyst, Glacier Vandervell, Inc. On-site interview, May 5-6.

Van Pelt, D. 1993. Manager, quality control, Glacier Vandervell, Inc. On-site interview, May 5-6.

8

Accounting Excellence Within a Large Corporate Environment

The CFO Organization at AT&T Power Systems

Introduction

AT&T Power Systems, located in Dallas, Texas, is one of five strategic business units in AT&T Microelectronics and is a world-class manufacturer of energy systems, electronic power supplies, and components for the data processing and telecommunications industries. A section of AT&T Bell Laboratories was moved from New Jersey to Dallas in 1989 to become part of Power Systems. This $600 million per year organization at present employs approximately 3,500 workers worldwide, 2,300 at the Dallas plant.

Success at Power Systems has come, to a great extent, as the result of state-of-the-art manufacturing capabilities and renowned research and development resources. In 1988, management began an initiative known as Dallas Vision to establish Power Systems as a world-class competitor by implementing total quality management and just-in-time (JIT) manufacturing methodologies. The Power Systems Quality Council was formed in 1990 to establish quality as the number one priority of the organization. The Quality Council established three imperatives: customer satisfaction, employee satisfaction, and stakeholder satisfaction. A key strategy for the successful implementation of the quality imperatives involves the empowerment of the Vision Implementation Through People (VIP) teams, special cross-functional groups formed to identify and eliminate problems in manufacturing processes.

The Power Systems initiatives have led to the following achievements:

➤ Average outgoing quality defects reduced by 70%,
➤ Rework reduced by 70%,

- First-pass yield increased from 87% to 95%,
- Inventory reduced by over 50%,
- Storeroom reduced by 100,000 square feet,
- Customer order interval reduced by 50%,
- New product introduction interval reduced up to 50%.

AT&T Power Systems was awarded the 1992 Shingo Prize for Excellence in American Manufacturing.

Organizational Change Within Power Systems

The massive restructuring of AT&T in the mid-1980s significantly changed the business orientation of this corporate giant. Business Unit Head William Yeates describes the evolution of the business unit within AT&T:

> We had one AT&T with all these factories throughout the world making products for AT&T. Then we broke that down into three businesses with sales volume of 10-15 billion dollars each. . . . We then broke that down into 20 businesses and underneath that we had SBUs [strategic business units], each SBU broken into internal business units [IBU] with a lot of focus on the direct product line. This has changed the way we've done accounting . . . I used to say that all of our systems were geared to give Bob Allen [AT&T chairman] the number first and then give us the number later. . . . All the money would roll up to the corporation and then they would "allocate" the money back down to the businesses.

Power Systems is in essence a "focused business unit." All its designers are in Dallas, as are all marketing and financial personnel. Their proximity allows these functions to interact frequently (Archer 1993).

Chief Financial Officer A. L. (Pete) Peterson has observed significant changes in the area of design for manufacturing (DFM). Years ago a product design would be mailed from Bell Labs in New Jersey to be built in Dallas. Typically, many changes had to be made in the design in Dallas to make the product manufacturable. Now, with Bell Labs located on site, the engineer must interact with the manufacturing personnel who will build the product and the marketing personnel who represent the product to the customer (Peterson 1993).

The Power Systems Manufacturing Environment

Power Systems used to have a storeroom in the middle of the factory to store work-in-process inventory. Individual functional departments could remove raw material, perform their part of the process, then return it to the storeroom and receive recovery (credit for a sale) when the transfer transaction was processed. Another department eventually would retrieve the work-in-process item from the storeroom and perform its operations. Because departments got credit as soon as they completed their operation and returned the item to inventory, their incentive was to build excess inventory. The transfer transactions were causing three problems:

- Departments would tend to build excess inventories of selected parts because they got immediate shipping credit upon transfer;
- The storage and transport of the excess inventory represented additional waste;
- Significant wasted effort was involved in entering and processing the transactions themselves.

Now, when inventory leaves the storeroom, it is not transferred back. A cell will work only on a component or assembly that is needed for a customer shipment. In addition, as Power Systems has moved to JIT, unnecessary transactions have been eliminated, particularly those involving the transfer of work-in-process between departments. Administrative Director John Archer observes:

> As you go to JIT you begin to realize that your in-process [inventory] is going down. You don't need to know where everything is because your cycle times are getting shorter and the materials are flowing through and you are doing a lot of unnecessary work [entering transfer transactions]. We eliminated all that. . . . The only time a shop knows that they are getting "paid" for a product is when the product ships. We call that backflushing (Archer 1993).

Eliminating the back-and-forth transfer of in-process parts from the storeroom also improves quality. For example, in the past, metal encasing panels might not match each other in color because the separate panels were painted weeks apart. The slight difference in paint shades would become obvious upon assembly and reflect on the quality of the product (Archer 1993).

■ Kanban at Power Systems

Prior to the JIT configuration, products and subassemblies were built to forecast. A computer printout would inform each department how many assemblies to build by the end of the week. In theory, by the end of the week enough of the correct assemblies would be available to build the forecast number of products. Archer remembers that too often key components were missing at assembly time because one or more departments did not build enough of the required assemblies or built the wrong one.

Now, the kanban system acts as a signaling mechanism that pulls the correct number of assemblies through the cells as customers require shipment.

The kanban technique also is used to authorize resupply of materials and parts. Laminated cards attached to the parts bins contain the part number, description, and kanban quantity in both text and bar-code format. When a kanban quantity is used up, a vendor can pick up the card from the bin, scan the bar code to make the purchase transaction, and return with the kanban card and replenishment parts to the receiving dock, at which point both are brought directly to the cell.

The Changing Financial Culture

Peterson has seen considerable change in the AT&T financial-management orientation in recent years. It used to be that top management would call at the end of the month ordering the business unit to reduce inventory or to complain that inventory was too high. Peterson notes that there are two ways to reduce inventory—junk it, or reduce outlays for new inventory. The former has an immediate effect on the bottom line. The latter will hit the bottom line more gradually as more sales are lost because of eventual shortages of the faster-moving inventory items. What upper management really wanted but did not ask for directly was to increase cash flow. Now, top management asks about cash flow, and inventory is an issue only as it pertains to increasing cash flow. He believes that the relevance of inventory now is not its present level but rather how many times inventory is being turned.

The need to know product-level incurred costs has increased as Power Systems has expanded beyond the captive market of the former Bell System. Peterson describes the cost accounting culture of AT&T prior to deregulation and divestiture:

> As part of the former Bell System, there was no justification for precision costing down to the bottom (individual product) level. Families of products, yes. But not individual products. It was okay because we were selling families of products and we were selling them as families to operating companies [within Bell]. So it didn't make a difference if you didn't know what widget A or widget B cost. But now we sell widget A to company A and widget B to company B. Now we need to know if we are making a profit on each one of those.

Yeates relates that his business unit recently applied activity-based costing to one production line. As the business unit began to obtain a clearer picture of the cost structures of some of their existing lines, they began to compare these cost structures with those of other businesses. "You start looking at other businesses and you discover, 'I could be in that business.' In the past I would look at my standard rate and it would make all my low-volume items look cheap . . . and all my high-volume product costs real high, where in reality it might be the opposite."

Yeates believes that activity-based costing can be an effective tool to reduce costs. Cost drivers that are identified can be managed. ABC can help drive out a manufacturer's less competitive products and indicate when it may be appropriate to subcontract parts or services.

Yeates notes that his business unit also has developed financial-reporting capabilities that will produce profit and loss statements by project. Managers and employees are better motivated because their operating performance is not buried in an aggregated reporting system.

Peterson distinguishes business management from budget management. He relates a story of a manager who was commended by the organization for underspending his budget by 2%. Unfortunately, his was a service department, and the division serviced by this department missed its revenue targets by 20%. Peterson notes that a major improvement in financial control has occurred by managing the business rather than the budget.

Power Systems IBUs had been operating as profit centers and were being allocated corporate overhead that used to be taken into account in the evaluation of the business units. Peterson relates that more time was being spent debating the appropriate overhead-allocation scheme than was being spent on strategies to increase contribution margins. A change was made to limit the evaluation of the IBUs to contribution margin and controllable expenses. Overhead was applied eventually but was not used for evaluation purposes. The result is that the business units can focus on the activities they can control.

■ Meeting the Demands of Financial Customers

According to Peterson, internal customers are calling for more information (as opposed to "data") and wanting it more quickly. Customers of the CFO organization expect proactive financial support. Accounting should be an indicator of what will happen tomorrow instead of what happened yesterday.

> Managers want to know how many orders were taken, did we ship on time, what was the cost to make the product, did the cost reduction work, did the new design come in at the cost that was projected for it? What do they need to work on to get the cost reductions? What everyone wants is enough information so that decisions are not required. In theory, with perfect information many decisions would not have to be made. With

perfect information on what product costs were and the knowledge of what drives those costs, a manager would know how resources could be applied to fix problems within a particular line. For example, it would be dumb to cost reduce a 3-cent screw when the most that could be hoped for would be a 2.9-cent screw. Also, it would be dumb to cost reduce a $100 device if only a hundred were called for a year (Peterson 1993).

Business Unit Head Vernell Guest (1993) points out that the CFO organization is customer oriented just as the business units are. She receives surveys from finance to assess the satisfaction of her business unit. She emphasizes that the same TQM principles that guide manufacturing are also applicable to the finance function.

■ From Controller to Advisor

Peterson believes that no financial officer should bear the title of "controller."

> I have a personal hang-up about the word "controller." That word to me is like saying "gotcha." . . . The objective used to be to catch somebody doing something wrong and point it out, as opposed to saying, "if you do it this way it will lessen the risk, improve the return, or shorten the cycle time." . . . There is a completely different flavor to the controllership function. . . . Unfortunately, here we are trying to overcome a history where the position has *demanded* rather than *offered* information.

Guest notes that four to five years ago internal financial reporting tended to be "rolled up from the bottom" and was focused to inform top management. She feels that internal information reporting is now focused more toward the operational business unit. She views this change as an improvement because the business units are in a position to react to such reporting.

The Power Systems CFO Organization

The financial and accounting arm of Power Systems, the CFO organization, is organized so that one of their business unit analysts (BUA) is dedicated to each business unit. The BUA is charged with working closely with the business unit head (BUH) to explain results, identify problems and potential solutions from a financial standpoint, conduct business case analysis (BCA) to evaluate business opportunities, and assist with financial forecasting. The BUA generally sits on the business unit management team. In most cases the BUAs are located physically within their business unit (Knight 1993).

The CFO Organization at AT&T Power Systems

The CFO organization has established a quality plan incorporating a set of well-defined initiatives that are directly linked to the three Power Systems global imperatives: improving customer satisfaction, employee satisfaction, and stakeholder satisfaction. For each CFO initiative, a management checkpoint (metric for assessing the achievement of an objective) has been developed. A target level of achievement is established and actual performance is measured against the target. Exhibit 8-1 shows an excerpt from this documentation. Each initiative is further broken down and assigned to members of the CFO lead team. Each responsibility represents a managing point with corresponding checkpoints. Metrics are established to assess how effectively responsibilities are discharged (see Exhibit 8-2).

Guest describes the finance function as being very much a matrix configuration in that each business unit has a BUA who receives guidance from both the BUH and the CFO. The BUA is integrated into the business unit operations and attends BU staff meetings. This interface allows the BUA to be closely attuned to information needs of that business unit. At the same time, the CFO organization exerts a counterbalancing force to

Exhibit 8-1. Quality Plan (excerpt)

Power Systems Imperatives	CFO Initiatives	Indicators	Target (Year)	Actual (Year)
Improve customer satisfaction	Business case coverage	% cases approved	____	____
	Customer report card	Development/ implementation	____	____
	•	•	•	•
	•	•	•	•
Improve employee satisfaction	TQM activities	# hours spent	____	____
	Team building	# hours spent	____	____
	•	•	•	•
	•	•	•	•
Improve stakeholder satisfaction	CFO productivity	Expense as revenue %	____	____
	•	•	•	•
	•	•	•	•

Exhibit 8-2. CFO Daily Work Management (excerpt)

Job Responsibility	Managing Point	When Measured	Checking Point	Target	When Measured	Person Responsible
Financial results	% complete by	Monthly	% complete by	95%	Monthly	IBU analyst
	...	...	...	...	...	...
Business case coverage	Delivered vs. reviewed	Monthly	Delivered & reviewed by IBU	90% < 48 hrs.	On-going	IBU analyst
	...	...	...	...	...	...
TQM implem.	% partic.	Monthly	% partic. by employee	75%/ 100%	Monthly	Quality facilitator
	...	...	...	...	...	...
Employee	Training hrs. per employee	Quarterly	Training hrs. per employee	40/year	Monthly	Quality facilitator

make sure that commonalities are present in financial reporting across Power Systems.

Guest believes that the physical location of BUAs within each business unit has been a success:

> When people don't sit next to you ... there is a tendency to view them as not being a part of your organization. Therefore, the business unit throws things over the fence to the financial community and the financial community throws things back over the fence to the business unit. One of our goals in placing [BUAs] in the business unit was to force the business unit heads to recognize that they are responsible for their business and they need to tell the financial community what they need to run their business. It's not the financial community's responsibility to guess what that is.

Peterson has observed a shift in direction from a corporation managing by financial mandate to one where local business units determine their own information needs:

> This is my third business unit. The first time I got involved in one of these, the financial organization drove the information flow ... to force business units to manage their business. In this one (Power Systems) ... the change was driven by the operating people. They demanded information.

■ The Business Unit Analyst

The BUA at Power Systems serves essentially as the CFO for the internal business unit to which he or she is assigned. John Case (1993), BUA, describes the role of this position: "The overriding focus of our function is to give the BUH ... advice on how to run his business."

Case points out that although a business unit may be generating millions of dollars in profits, some product lines are a drag on the bottom line and need to be identified. He relates that the business unit he supported was suffering significant losses. Analysis by his financial team revealed that the losses were caused almost entirely by a single customer. Case observes that while such a problem would seem to be obvious to the BUH, in this case it was overlooked because the reporting did not at that time focus on such exceptions. Now, reporting is available at a code-specific level in addition to having Pareto analysis of customers. The new reporting strategy is to highlight problem areas for the BUH.

Yeates emphasizes that his production people are experts at running a factory but not at understanding financial matters. Yeates believes that management accounting's role is to help the BUs understand the financial consequences of their actions. In other words, what are the business drivers behind the financial results?

BUA Greg Lynch (1993) observes that financial presentations to engineers and production personnel must be geared to their business perspective. For example, in explaining the implications of the return on capital measurement, more understanding is imparted if it is expressed as inventory levels or overtime percentages.

Kevin Mortazavi, senior financial planner, marketing and sales, serves as liaison between the CFO organization and the sales organization. He views part of his role as playing the "devil's advocate" to his BU by asking the difficult questions. He emphasizes that he is not simply being an impediment. His role is viewed very positively by his constituents because the business unit is relatively new and is under constant scrutiny by top management. Mortazavi makes sure that his business unit is considering all relevant information for its planning and strategy and can withstand this additional scrutiny.

The BUA is relied on not only to interpret historical financial information but to advise the BUH on future-oriented financial impacts. In this regard, Mortazavi views his time perspective somewhat differently from the traditional historical view of accounting. He stated, "In any given month, I spend three days looking back and twenty days looking forward."

■ Business Case Analysis

One of the most significant proactive products of the CFO organization is the business case analysis, a formal methodology used to evaluate the financial impact of major new business opportunities. According to Peterson:

> We don't spend any money without a business case—any new venture—any major capital acquisition. The purpose of the business case is not to determine if there is a reasonable return on the investment. That's the best way to guarantee mediocrity forever. What it says is . . . this is the magnitude of the risk.

Business case analysis was developed and continues to be driven by the CFO organization. They compile the financial information, the assumptions, and the narrative that make up the business case. The parties involved in developing the business case include the BUAs and representatives from sales (customers), engineering, purchasing, production manager, and finance. The business case may involve the input of between 20 to 30 people (Mortazavi 1993).

The business case methodology used at Power Systems involves four analytical stages:

Discovery stage. In the discovery stage, the business opportunity or problem is identified. The business case team then considers the strategic fit of the opportunity and how it relates to the existing business. They try to develop short-term and long-term objectives and then draft an initial proposal for review.

Framing stage. In framing the business case, team members raise issues such as customer needs, competitive position, technology, and cost regulation. At this stage, they gather facts and reach consensus on the underlying assumptions, proposed alternatives, uncertainties, composition of the business case team, and review and evaluation process.

Analysis stage. In the analysis stage, the business case team researches viable alternatives and performs the appropriate analyses of cash flow, net present value, and economic sensitivity. They prepare the rationale for the recommended course of action and present documentation of results to the decision board.

Connection stage. The planning for implementation occurs at the connection stage. Responsibilities and commitments are delineated, budgets outlined, and a tracking plan devised. The business case then is submitted for final approval.

The CFO organization makes every effort not to use business cases as limiters. According to Peterson, "if you are going to bet the farm . . . you have to evaluate how much you have at risk . . . and you have to put some checkpoints in place to avoid losing the whole farm."

■ Measurements and Metrics

A major management accounting challenge is the effective use of measurement both to motivate employees and to gauge performance. According to Peterson:

> The biggest problem in management accounting . . . is understanding the behavior your measurements are going to drive. There never was a problem with measuring efficiency. Efficiency is a perfectly legitimate measure of performance. The problem is that people will scope in on a single metric, whatever it might be. No single metric is appropriate. If you measure efficiency, then you have to measure inventory turns, customer service, and aggregate cost. If you just measure efficiency, you *will* destroy yourself. When you put a metric in place, you must be careful also to put a countermetric in place to prevent the first metric from causing stupidity.

Yeates sees an important role for management accounting in the selection of meaningful metrics to drive proper behavior in the business. He notes, for example, that engineering personnel are being encouraged to design more standardized parts into new products. "What you are trying to point out to people is . . . just because it is gee-whiz technology doesn't mean it is better for the business."

Yeates points out that there is a significant cost to buy these unique parts and additional costs to maintain them. To give incentive to use standard parts, a project may be charged $2,000 for each new part number introduced into a design. Incentives such as this have helped change design behavior. Formerly, 20% of the designs were in compliance with the standard parts guidelines. Now, 80% of the designs are in compliance.

Peterson points out that every time a new part is added, both risk and cost increase. He observes that AT&T has a world-renowned R&D community. Their reward mechanisms used to be based on producing patents for high-technology products. There was never a reward mechanism for the design of a commercially profitable, long-lived product. However, since the partial relocation of Bell Laboratories to the Dallas plant, these reward mechanisms have been reengineered to favor viable, profitable products.

■ Broadening Accounting Horizons

Mortazavi believes that finance personnel should be rotated through the shop floor to allow them to see what it takes to make the product and what manufacturing personnel need to know to function in their jobs. He emphasizes that accountants should understand the business processes, not just the financial perspectives. [At the time of this interview, Mortazavi was scheduled to begin a manufacturing rotation that will last two years.] "I think that is the biggest shortcoming we have in finance . . . that sometimes we don't want to take our tie off and get involved."

Mortazavi observes that it is easy to tell which accountants have operational experience.

> When I approach those financial people [those with operational experience] I always come away with a complete understanding of the process. When I go to a purely financial person who hasn't been out there, I can tell the difference. They know their job . . . but they don't have a clear picture of the overall situation . . . [Broadening financial personnel] will give finance more credibility. It's a lot easier for me to meet with a BUH and talk about productivity when they know I have been out there and that I know what they are talking about. They will probably buy in to my recommendations or to what I'm saying more readily than they would someone who has been in the office the whole time.

Implications for Management Accounting

1. Management and finance must consider the disincentives and waste that may be generated by recording interdepartmental production transactions, particularly in a JIT environment. JIT production methods translate into much shorter manufacturing cycle times and lower inventory levels. In such an environment, there is less need to maintain detailed transactions on product movement and status. Moreover, products are likely to have shipped before the transactions can be processed and analyzed. The effort spent by production workers recording such transactions and the effort of accountants to process and interpret the data may not be returning the expected benefits.

A more sinister by-product of some types of in-process transactions is the incentive for local optimization. If an internal production department is allowed to "book" a sale or receive equivalent credit for processing activities not directly related to an actual customer shipment, incentives may inadvertently be created to build excess inventory. This situation will have implications for most inventory in-process transfer schemes as well as for transfer pricing mechanisms.

2. *Accountants must differentiate between business management and budget management.* Accounting constituents now are expecting much more from their financial advisor than enforcing budget compliance. Naturally, accountants must be careful that their budgeting schemes do not invite abuse or punish responsible business management. But more important, the accounting function must provide the financial advisory support that cell managers need to manage their businesses intelligently.

3. *Accounting initiatives should be linked directly with corporate initiatives and provide a management checkpoint for measuring their achievement.* The success of the Shingo Prize recipients is in large measure due to the integration of continuous improvement methodologies throughout the organization, including service units such as accounting. Just as manufacturing cells link their operations to organizational goals and faithfully measure their performance against operational checkpoints, accounting likewise must assure that its processes are consistent with organizational imperatives. Accordingly, measures should demonstrate that accounting processes are producing quality output and that accounting responsibilities are being discharged effectively.

4. *The accounting function should be physically close to the operation it supports.* Power Systems has benefited by the physical placement of the BUA within the BU. This arrangement has the obvious benefits of daily contact with operating personnel, participation in BU staff meetings, and a better understanding of the operating environment. These benefits should lead to increased trust between accounting and operating functions and better insights into the kinds of accounting information needed to support operations.

5. *The accounting organization should consider the benefits of a formal business case methodology to support major business decision making.* Organizations often must consider significant business opportunities and would

benefit from a methodology that lends rigor and structure to the evaluation process. The Power Systems CFO organization has assumed the lead in the application of this methodology, and as a result has placed itself in a key role in major business decisions. While the methodology is rigorous, the CFO organization is careful that the business case is not used as a limiter but as an important tool to assess risk.

Conclusion

AT&T Microelectronics Power Systems has demonstrated that large manufacturers can make an effective transition to lean manufacturing. The Power Systems CFO organization likewise has made a transition from an environment of top-down, financially driven directives to an environment of operating-level business unit support. Finance stays close to its constituents by placing business unit analysts physically within the manufacturing units. Also, finance enjoys an enhanced stature throughout Power Systems with the visibility of the business case methodology.

References

Archer, J.W. 1993. Administrative director, AT&T Power Systems. On-site visit, April 29-30.

Case, J. 1993. Business planning and analysis manager, AT&T Power Systems. On-site visit, April 29-30.

Guest, V. 1993. Business unit head, energy systems, AT&T Power Systems. On-site visit, April 29-30.

Knight, K. 1993. Business planning and analysis manager, AT&T Power Systems. On-site visit, April 29-30.

Lynch, G. 1993. Business planning and analysis manager, AT&T Power Systems. On-site visit, April 29-30.

Mortazavi, K. 1993. Senior financial planner, business planning and analysis, AT&T Power Systems. On-site visit, April 29-30.

Peterson, A.L. 1993. Chief financial officer, AT&T Power Systems. On-site visit, April 29-30.

Yeates, W.T. 1993. Business unit head, off-line switchers, AT&T Power Systems. On-site visit, April 29-30.

9

Manufacturing Excellence Through Systems Integration
Lifeline Systems, Inc.

Introduction

Lifeline Systems, Inc. is the industry leader in the field of personal emergency response systems. Founded in 1974, Lifeline is not only a manufacturer of emergency monitoring systems but also a provider of real-time monitoring services to elderly subscribers.

Lifeline's commitment to continuous improvement began in 1987 when the company changed from a work order, batch processing environment to continuous flow manufacturing (CFM). Lifeline's achievements have included:

- 400% increase in use of floor space;
- Reduction of product lead time from 30 days in 1987 to less than five days;
- Development of a virtually paperless purchasing system;
- Elimination of all in-process inspection activity;
- Transfer of all off-shore manufacturing to a single domestic plant;
- Increase of 255% in units produced per manufacturing employee;
- Reduction of credit memoranda from 5% to .5% of revenue;
- Establishment of supplier certification program to reduce suppliers from over 300 in 1987-1988 to 75 today.

In recognition of these achievements, Lifeline was honored in May 1991 as the small business recipient of the Shingo Prize for Excellence in American Manufacturing.

■ The Q[10] Initiative

To understand the continuous improvement culture at Lifeline Systems, Inc., one must consider their total quality management philosophy, known throughout the company as Q^{10}. This notation is designed as a reminder to employees that every process could be improved by a factor of 10 each year. Q^{10} consists of four broad concepts:

- The recognition that total quality management is the key to customer satisfaction,
- Continuous improvement,
- The elimination of errors through visibility,
- The belief that all errors are preventable.

To bring these concepts to the consciousness of the production workers, in conspicuous locations Lifeline has posted charts describing both the "friends" and "enemies" of Q^{10}. They are reproduced in Exhibits 9-1 and 9-2.

Quality consciousness has permeated the entire organization. According to Operations Vice President John Gugliotta (1991), "world-class quality will be attained only when continuous improvement philosophies extend into all departments within an organization." Gugliotta (1993) sums up Lifeline's continuous improvement initiative as follows: "If every person on the production floor gets two percent smarter this year, we gain a person by the end of the year."

System Integration — System Reliance

John Giannetto (1993), corporate manager–materials and purchasing, attributes much of Lifeline's success to their commitment to a *single* integrated information system that allows managers to monitor and con-

Exhibit 9-1. Friends of Q^{10} (Lifeline Systems, Inc.)

The customer is first.
Continuous improvement is essential to success.
Quality doesn't take time, it saves time.
What gets measured gets managed.
Problems are opportunities in disguise.
The only bad mistake is a hidden mistake.
Training saves money.
It's the process, not the people.
Better is better than best.
We're all in this together.
If we don't do it first, someone else will.

Exhibit 9-2. Enemies of Q^{10} (Lifeline Systems, Inc.)

It's the best we can do.
There's not enough time.
There's not enough money.
There aren't enough people.
It's not in MY budget.
It's not MY responsibility.
Let someone else worry about it.
It's too late to change it.
The customer doesn't understand; it's not REALLY a problem.
It's not my fault.
The QC stuff only applies to Manufacturing.
It's as good as it can be.
Relax . . . We hit the goal.

---

trol manufacturing processes as well as understand and control product costs. Giannetto believes that 95% of the processes must be maintained under the control of the system, so management is free to focus on the remaining 5% of exceptions.

■ Plain Vanilla Please . . . and Hold the Chocolate Chips

Despite the many "flavors" of information systems that Lifeline might have selected, developed, or customized, it has been the "vanilla" system that has appealed to their top management. The vanilla system of choice is the ASK MAN software for integrated manufacturing and accounting. This package runs on the DEC VAX platform and is also available for Hewlett-Packard hardware.

Giannetto emphasizes that Lifeline did not tailor the software to the company. Rather, their philosophy has been to change what they were doing to fit the system. ". . . We kept it in its 'vanilla' state. We never added a chocolate chip unless that was the only way we could get through. . . . We kept the exceptions down to the point that if we were asking for something the system couldn't do, we would ask ourselves why we were asking that question. We either changed what we were asking or we got to the point where we had to add the chocolate chips."

James Dillon (1993), manager of production and manufacturing engineering, adds:

We will adjust ourselves to fit the system as much as possible, and therefore be better able to use it to its fullest capabilities. Because today's software has so much flexibility, why wouldn't we want to optimize and take advantage of all the flexibility available? Mostly, because you lose the ability to maintain full enterprise integration. This has always been a priority.... Every part of the organization should know what the other parts are doing. An organization is only as strong as its weakest link.

The vanilla system philosophy departs from traditional systems development wisdom whereby users are assumed to know what their systems needs are and reserve the right to customize features that complement their work habits. However, these assumptions are not necessarily defensible. System users may only be reinventing the new system to allow them to continue with familiar work patterns. Customizing can create excess baggage when it comes time for routine software updates; in many cases the customizing has to be reimplemented continually with each new release. Furthermore, unnecessary customizing is likely to prevent the organization from taking advantage of the features that are part of the system, features developed through years of experience with a wide variety of manufacturers. As Gugliotta (1993) points out, "If the system we have can't answer the questions, go back and check the question. Maybe you're asking the wrong question . . . the ASK system has probably been installed in 5,000 companies in the United States and has gone through many updates."

■ Ownership of the Corporate Database

Lifeline places strong emphasis on a centralized database approach based on the ASK MAN manufacturing and accounting software. Data integrity and system reliability are absolutely essential because all departments obtain their data from the same database system. To be able to trust the system, users must be well trained in input procedures and understand the impact of the data they are entering on other departments within the company. When Cost Accounting Supervisor Bill Bogner (1993) discovers a data input error, he immediately briefs the originator on the downstream effect of that error. Bogner believes that once employees understand how their functions tie into the organization, they take more responsibility for their actions and are more likely to view themselves as an integral part of the organization rather than a task performer.

■ Integrated Systems and Autopilots

Although Lifeline strives to bring processes under control of the system (95/5 rule) and expects the people to trust the system, Gugliotta emphasizes that someone will always check the system output to make sure it feels right. Gugliotta tells of an exchange he had with a former employer in which the boss said, "You know, as soon as we have this computer system up we'll be able to run it with a bunch of clerks." Gugliotta replied, "That's like saying that once we buy one of these modern airplanes, we can let the flight attendants fly it."

Gugliotta prefers to compare the integrated system to the autopilot of a Boeing 747 passenger jet. Even though the autopilot may at times be controlling the plane, the pilot is still there, alert and ready for override in case a problem is encountered.

■ Dollars vs. Units: Sharing Responsibility for System Integrity

System outputs are expressed both in quantities and in dollars. At Lifeline, if a reported number has a dollar sign in front of it, accounting is responsible for it. On the other hand, if the output is in terms of quantities or other nonfinancial measures, operations is responsible for its integrity (Giannetto 1993). This concept is more than a simplistic division of labor. Quantities, times, ratios, and other nonfinancial measures represent the state of manufacturing operations at a point in time. Operations personnel should be in the best position to verify that those measures accurately reflect the existing operational states. Accounting, on the other hand, must be able to measure the financial impact of actions taking place on the production line.

Translating operational measures into a meaningful financial impact remains a challenging problem. Nevertheless, top management at Lifeline is advancing the notion that workers must know about business profitability. They believe that measures of that profitability must be taken down to the level of direct labor. Furthermore, the employee at the direct-labor level must be able to influence (but not necessarily control) that measurable activity (Giannetto 1993).

■ Paperless Internal Systems: Death of the Five-Part PO

Giannetto relates that Lifeline formerly used a purchase order with carbons that generated five copies. Each of the copies was filed in each of five locations. They have entirely eliminated the use of this business document. Orders are placed by phone with the supplier. Purchasing enters this communication with the supplier directly into the system (items, terms, delivery schedule). Receiving records shipment directly into the system (no paper receiving report is issued). Finally, payments are issued through the system.

■ Measuring Processes

An important tenet of the Q^{10} philosophy at Lifeline is measuring the process, making the measurements visible, and taking corrective action for problems (Giannetto 1993). Tight systems integration facilitates the measurement process at Lifeline:

> Back in 1987-88, credit memos issued per month totaled $250,000. Measures were taken to determine the causes of the credits. These measures were posted in the form of Pareto graphs for everyone to see. By focusing attention on these problems, credits have been reduced to between $25,000 and $50,000 per month.

Q^{10} from an Accounting Perspective

How is the spirit of Q^{10} manifested in the accounting function? Gugliotta emphasizes that the primary job of the finance function is not merely to report what happened, rather, "one of the functions of any finance organization is to educate the world around them . . . how their activities affect the profits of the organization." According to Giannetto, an important indication is the degree to which accounting facilitates forward-looking information support. He has seen a shift in the emphasis on historical reporting in the last few years. Fifteen years ago management might have spent 75% of its financial analysis effort on historical data and 25% on future-oriented analysis. He feels this ratio is now reversed, with 75% of the emphasis placed on future-oriented data without becoming overly obsessed with the accuracy of those data.

■ Facilitator vs. Gatekeeper

Lifeline Controller Robert Bowdring (1993) attributes much of the success of Lifeline's accounting function to having dismantled the stereotype of finance being the "bad guys"—the people who come in at the end of the decision-making process to announce that something cannot be done. At Lifeline, finance gets involved in the decision process up front to assess the point of view of each stakeholder. This method avoids unpleasant surprises at the end of the decision process.

■ Relaxing Accounting Boundaries

Territorial claims formerly held exclusively by accounting have given way to some extent to other functional departments. For example, Lifeline's costing system provides three fields for the recording of product costs: standard cost, current cost (last purchase divided by number of units purchased), and proposed cost. Formerly, accounting was the only department allowed access to these fields. Now, departments such as manufacturing and engineering are allowed access to the current-cost and proposed-cost fields for the purpose of conducting "what-if" analyses. Because standard cost is the basis for the financial reporting system, accounting maintains control over that field. Far from being simply a turf concession, accounting now has access to cost computations made by the other departments, which formerly were not part of the system. Accounting now can evaluate this prospective cost information and compare it with present standards. This access gives accounting the opportunity to offer suggestions (for example, a part substitution) or spot potential errors (Bowdring 1993, Bogner 1993).

Innovative Accounting Support at Lifeline

■ Accountant, Measure Thyself

Generally, the accounting function is not involved in developing nonfinancial measures for operational monitoring. Like all functional departments, they compile nonfinancial measures for their own processes. For example, a measure of the effectiveness of the paperless purchasing system is the number of manual checks written. Lifeline wants to eliminate this activity because it costs much more to write a check manually than to process it through the system. Another nonvalue-added activity performed by accounting is the month-end close, so the length of the closing process is measured and reported with the intent to reduce the closing duration (Giannetto 1993).

■ Continuous Flow and Reduced Transaction Detail

Bogner describes the changes that occurred when Lifeline changed from a work order-driven manufacturing process to a continuous flow manufacturing process. Under the work order system, accounting was heavily involved with detailed transaction recording. For example, they expended much effort obtaining accurate time measures for each work order. With the repetitive approach, effort was shifted from detailed hourly labor transaction processing to support of a backflush approach.

■ Backflush Cost Transfers

Bowdring describes the integration of the ASK MAN order entry system with the backflush cost transfer. After the finished unit is packed, the bar code on the box is scanned by wand just before loading onto the delivery truck. Data identified by the bar code include customer ID, product ID, and customized programming codes. The bar code wanding process accomplishes the following steps:

- Effectively backflushes the cost of the product;
- Sets up a transaction in the system indicating that a product has been shipped but not invoiced;
- Triggers the issuance of the invoice.

■ Activity-Based Costing

Lifeline has experimented with reevaluating standard costs based on ABC. This approach is used at present to understand costing structures. The company hopes to gain a better understanding of what is driving the costs so as to control them better.

Although Lifeline has been involved in ABC to some extent for the last four years, Bogner believes that a more extensive use of ABC is not cost effective for a single-product-line company such as Lifeline. The ASK MAN system does not presently offer an integrated ABC capability. Consequently, maintaining such a system would take a significant commitment.

■ Strategic Decision Support — Offshore Manufacturing

Prior to 1988, 50% of Lifeline's manufacturing operation was offshore (Korea). The company successfully eliminated their offshore operations and, with the implementation of JIT, the domestic facility absorbed the additional offshore production without additional staff or floor space.

Lifeline had several problems associated with the foreign operation. First, the company experienced higher freight costs and delays attributed to customs compliance and complex logistics. Second, the offshore operation was vulnerable to political instability. Third, new product start-up times abroad are typically twice as long as with domestic operations. Fourth, it is more difficult to control quality in offshore operations. Failure rates for offshore production were running 15 to 20%. (Upon repatriation, the failure rate dropped to 5% and is now 3%.) Finally, it takes much longer to react to engineering changes. By the time the engineering change order (ECO) was received by the Korean contractor, 4,000 units might already be in the pipeline (Giannetto 1993).

Accounting was actively involved in the decision process that terminated the Korean operations. Accounting pointed out that it was costing three times as much to produce the units offshore as it would cost to produce them domestically (Bowdring 1992, Bogner 1993). The Watertown plant was able to absorb the additional output formerly built in Korea by carefully examining the labor-intensive processes and improving those efficiencies. For example, cutting, bending, and soldering leads used to be a time-consuming process that was improved by buying the leads already cut and bent.

■ Replacing Physical Inventory with Cycle Counts

Bowdring relates that six years ago inventories were taken every quarter, shutting down production for four to five days each quarter. Since 1990, cycle counting has replaced the traditional physical inventory. External auditors now rely entirely on cycle counts and have learned to take a more systemic approach to the audit. Bowdring observes that traditional hard-copy auditing has been declining as increased emphasis is placed on the integrity of the system.

■ Reducing Invoice Copies

Lifeline has taken steps to eliminate nonvalue-added activities triggered by the handling of paper documents. For example, extra copies of invoices used to be printed out. One was filed in the customer file just in case the customer needed another copy. If the customer did ask for it, someone had to search for it, retrieve it, make a copy of it, and send it out. This copy was discontinued, thus eliminating the need to collate, sort, and insert the copy into the customer file. In addition, two invoice copies used to be sent to the customer. The company observed that the customer seldom sent back a copy of the invoice with the payment. Therefore, the company decided to discontinue the extra copy to the customer (Bowdring 1993, Bogner 1993).

■ Paperless Purchasing

The shift from a paper-driven purchasing system to an in-house paperless system saved one full-time equivalent (FTE) in accounting. This translates into an annual savings of $30,000 to $40,000 (Bowdring 1993).

■ Study of Credit Memorandums

A study of the source of credit memos showed that many customer returns occurred because the customer was ordering the wrong merchandise. These errors apparently were occurring because the customer typically did not have access to a catalog that showed a picture of the product, description of features, and item numbers. A catalog was prepared to reduce this type of mistake. The lesson learned from this example is that processes should be studied to determine the most common type of error and its cause (Bowdring 1993, Bogner 1993).

■ Providing Payables Visibility

On a monthly basis, accounting provides all departments with data on payable transactions. This report gives the departments an opportunity to see how they are spending their resources. It also serves as a control function, making sure the payable amounts resulted from materials or services ordered by them (Bowdring 1993, Bogner 1993).

- **Repairs Incident Reporting**

Formerly, all parts used in the repair of a product were recorded in connection with an incident report (tracking for individual product repair). Finance recognized that an enormous amount of time was spent keying in these parts. This method was slowing down the process and requiring more time to understand how many repairs were being done. Finally, finance compiled a list of low-cost parts for which data entry was not required. The outcome was very little information loss due to reduced tracking but large savings in the area of data input, shorter repair cycle time, and faster reporting response time (Bowdring 1993, Bogner 1993).

- **Month-End Close**

Month-end close procedures are now conducted over weekends to minimize disruption of the manufacturing process. Formerly, the close process required two to three days during which current transactions stacked up waiting for the completion of closing procedures (Bowdring 1993, Bogner 1993).

- **Accountant for a Day**

During a 1992 slowdown, the production line was experiencing idle time. Production workers noticed that while they sat mostly idle, employees in the administrative functions (including accounting) still appeared to be very busy. This situation motivated manufacturing workers to ask if they could assist with some of the administrative work. As a result, finance brought in many of the idled line workers rather than hire temporary clerical employees. A positive side effect of this arrangement was that the production workers became more familiar with the administrative functions and gained a greater appreciation of the administrative services being provided (Bowdring 1993, Bogner 1993).

- **Streamlining Travel Reimbursement**

Accounting has simplified (and shortened) the travel-reimbursement cycle for employees who travel. Employees check in with accounting just prior to departure and obtain a travel authorization code and a password to access the dial-up reimbursement system. As soon as the employee returns (even over weekends) he or she can dial up the reimbursement system, enter the appropriate codes, passwords, and expense account numbers and dollar amounts. The reimbursement is made by direct deposit within three days. Hard-copy documentation is then audited for compliance. Any errors are adjusted in the following reimbursement cycle. Two major benefits are associated with this approach. First, employee morale is improved because of the timely reimbursement. Second, the impact of travel expenses is known on a more timely basis. As a result, expenses are better matched to the appropriate time period (Bowdring 1993).

■ Right vs. Left Side of the Decimal

At Lifeline, the precision of accounting data is maintained to the penny. However, summary presentations are another matter. As Bowdring points out, "If you report in pennies and decimal points, people are going to focus on that" (Bowdring 1993, Bogner 1993). Gugliotta (1993) adds, "No matter what anyone tells you, there isn't an operations person in the world who will use more than the left two digits in any decision. . . . Everything else is trivial."

■ Process Improvement — Packaging

Products used to be packed in the shipping room prior to transit. Accounting suggested that packaging not only should be considered part of the product cost, but the packaging process should be included as part of the production process. Furthermore, it was determined that for the last half of the production process, the product did not need to be turned and therefore could rest in its protective styrofoam cocoon during the last steps of the process. The packaging actually assisted in stabilizing the product for those remaining processes (Bowdring 1993, Bogner 1993).

■ Participation in Engineering Changes

Lifeline's finance department, along with manufacturing, marketing, engineering, and service, participates in the approval of the engineering change order. In these situations, accounting may have the opportunity to point out the financial impact of a part change on existing parts inventories, for example, a stocked part becomes obsolete (Bowdring 1993, Bogner 1993).

■ Customer Satisfaction Measures

Accounting administers a comprehensive customer satisfaction survey that measures perceived product quality and satisfaction with customer service (including billing and collections). Another program has been initiated that gives Lifeline employees with customer contacts the authority to award appropriate compensation to customers who have had problems with Lifeline products or services. Such complaints are further analyzed to see if the identified deficiencies also may have been an issue with other customers who do not happen to complain (Bowdring 1993, Bogner 1993).

Future Challenges and Opportunities for Accounting

■ External Reporting Constraints

According to Bowdring, external reporting requirements to some extent have frustrated the innovative processes in management accounting. Not only do these requirements discourage the reporting of new types of accounting measures (Bowdring cites ABC as an example), but they require considerable accounting resources to support. Smaller companies such as Lifeline struggle with limited accounting resources to comply with statutory requirements and, at the same time, to develop more proactive, value-added accounting methods.

■ Thoughts on Benchmarking

Giannetto believes that accounting must focus on the operational aspects of benchmarking. He believes that a metric should indicate progress toward eliminating nonvalue-added activities. Rather than asking, "How many activities are you doing?" it should be asking, "How well are you doing those activities?" For example, rather than measuring the number of line items in the inventory, an accountant should measure the number of production days lost to take physical inventory. Instead of measuring the number of employees supported by payroll services, the ratio of employees to payroll staff could be computed. Giannetto believes the key question to be asked is, "Which measurement will help you understand what the process is doing?" For example, he suggests that rather than measuring the number of expense reports processed, measure the number of reports processed without error. Instead of measuring how many products are produced, measure the number of products produced per employee.

■ Reducing the Need for Auditors

What impact will organizational philosophies such as Q^{10} have on audit practice? Gugliotta (1993) directly addresses the auditing profession in the following quotation: "We've made your job easier. . . . It should be easier for you to audit us. Therefore, you should be here fewer days and charge us less money. We want you to tell us why you have to be here to audit some of these things or why you can't come during the year to audit some of the processes we use as opposed to auditing the numbers at the end of the year."

Gugliotta (1993) compares the audit profession to the quality profession in that many people in the quality world do not have the systems skills to audit the process. Consequently, they tend to want to look at the end result rather than at the processes themselves.

■ Challenging the Accounting System

Progression toward world-class manufacturing status appears to have been made at Lifeline by continually challenging existing wisdom and entrenched practices. Gugliotta (1993) relates that accounting practices also have come under scrutiny:

> We have challenged the way people use their timesheets. We have challenged the way people move the product around. We have challenged inventory transactions and the reason we need them. We have challenged filing systems. We have challenged why we need a purchase order to buy something.

Gugliotta also points out that organizations have failed to exploit the capabilities of modern information systems.

> Most companies who have put in a computer system today have forgotten one major piece. They have forgotten to update the manual systems. Accountants are probably the worst ones. They still want a copy of the transaction ticket. They want a copy of the purchase order, a copy of the invoice, a copy of the receiving ticket . . . You don't need most of that stuff if you have a system in place. . . . We eliminate a lot of source documents when we do backflushing after the fact.

Gugliotta is particularly critical of information systems that place more emphasis on historical information retrieval than on forward-looking analysis. He relates:

> At one time we had multiple copies of everything. We used to file copies of source documents by name, by number, by date. We had files for everything. One day I kind of blew up and said, "This is dumb, folks. Let's start focusing on making systems that go forward faster rather than systems that go backwards."

Gugliotta believes that the system should actually discourage employees from spending their time "going backwards" through past records.

■ Expanding the Horizons of Activity-based Costing

Gugliotta points out that in a company such as Lifeline, the opportunities for exploiting ABC may be greater if they are applied below the

Exhibit 9-3. ABC Company

	% CGS	% Revenue	%
Revenue			100
CGS:			
Labor	5.0	1.5	
Material	60.0	18.0	
Overhead	35.0	10.5	
	100.0	30.0	% 30
Gross margin			% 70

gross margin line on the income statement. He provides an illustration based on assumptions shown in Exhibit 9-3, a portion of a pro forma common unit (percentage-based) income statement representative of Lifeline Systems.

According to Gugliotta, an ABC system that focuses entirely on manufacturing overhead costs "slices and dices" 10.5% of a company's revenues and allocates it across the products. Furthermore, a portion of this overhead is noncontrollable in the short term. As a result, even less of the 10.5% is manageable. Gugliotta suggests that a greater payoff could be attained with ABC by applying it below the CGS line where 70% of revenues are at risk.

■ Limitations of ROI Computations

Gugliotta has often observed limitations of ROI computations related to capital equipment acquisitions. He relates that typically the proposal sponsor will present the acquisition proposal with accompanying analytical support showing how much the company supposedly will save. He suggests that two questions need to be asked:

1. Will we be saving money by buying this piece of equipment because it will eliminate labor costs?

2. *(If the answer to 1 is "yes")* What are the names of the employees who will lose their jobs the same day the machine arrives?

If the answer to question 2 is not known, the company is unlikely to be saving money. Another question that must be addressed is whether the new machine will get products out the door faster for the plant as a whole, not whether an individual production cell will achieve higher performance (Gugliotta 1993).

■ Identifying Excess Capacity

Gugliotta disagrees with the notion of keeping the production line balanced. On the contrary, he believes that operations must continually try to unbalance the line by identifying the bottleneck operation and making it the fastest operation, at which point the process is repeated with the next bottleneck that emerges.

He does not believe that the information system can effectively identify capacity differentials. Instead, he feels that managers must see and feel them by leaving their offices and observing their production lines.

■ Expense the Inventory?

One obvious result of JIT is the decline in the levels of inventory that need to be maintained to support the production line. Also, as cycle times have declined, it may be counterproductive to track inventory movement, added labor, and overhead absorption. Gugliotta observes:

> If you move material fast enough, it is not value-added to track it.... The inventory has gotten so low that I have tried to convince people to expense it when it arrives. Why take it, carry it, and drag it through the plant, drag it into finished goods, and drag it through the standard cost and the overhead absorption? Instead, expense it at the back door and you're done. For a million dollars last year we could have expensed the entire inventory of the plant and eliminated the whole cost accounting department. There is no value in it [product cost absorption]. All you are doing is delaying an expense. I call it financial gymnastics. You are delaying the expense of the people. You are delaying the expense of the parts, . . . and you are spending millions of dollars to perpetuate it (Gugliotta 1993).

The Lifeline Experience—Discussion and Implications

1. *Accountants must develop methods to measure the prospective financial impact of employee actions.* It is no longer sufficient for accountants to present the financial results of operations in retrospect. For financial reporting to be useful for motivational purposes, employees must understand the impact their actions have on the profitability of the company. This will require that accountants identify the correlation between operational measures and their corresponding financial results and be able to communicate these relationships in a straightforward, concise manner to managers and workers.

2. *Accountants must reevaluate the benefits of traditional costing measurements in light of modern manufacturing processes.* Reductions in manufacturing cycle times and the implementation of JIT systems have reduced the need for much of the detailed transaction processing associated with tracking work-in-process inventories. In many production environments, the product is produced and shipped in such a short period of time that the effort to record and process transactions pertaining to material usage, labor hours, and overhead absorption is literally wasted. In plants such as Lifeline's Watertown facility, a backflush approach is used to relieve materials inventory at the point of shipment. In any event, accountants must be alert to changing manufacturing methods and the impact they have on the relevance of costing systems.

3. *Accountants must use modern computer technology properly and dismantle the manual and paper-intensive systems the technology is supposed to replace.* The implementation of a modern computer system offers an excellent opportunity to reexamine manual and paper-intensive systems and reassign such clerical duties to the computer. Accountants continue to be criticized for holding on to familiar work patterns, in many cases under the guise of internal control concerns or mistrust of the system. Accountants must recognize that the maintenance of unnecessary paper trails not only prevents the full use of computer capability but also generates yet other nonvalue-added activities. To come to trust the system, accountants must have the systems skills necessary to evaluate it.

4. *The accounting and auditing professions must reevaluate procedural artifacts that hinder business productivity while producing questionable value.* Accountants should question the benefit of any accounting or auditing procedure that causes the business to work around it. For example, Lifeline has substituted cycle counting for the traditional physical inventory. The old procedure required the production line to be shut down for several days each quarter to accommodate it. Similarly, production workers used to be required to complete detailed labor reports to generate work-in-process transactions. Presently, cost transfers are accomplished ex post facto through the backflush system. Month-end close is another opportunity for streamlining. The accounting system must not be allowed to delay the entry or processing of transactions for the new operating period.

5. *Bring operations under control of a single integrated system—and trust that system.* This admonition applies as much to the accounting and auditing functions as to operations. Accountants and auditors should have the expertise to evaluate the integrity of the information system. Once they have done so, they should rely on it. Their activities should focus on the processes of the system. The creation of custom "shadow" systems should be viewed with skepticism. From the

auditing perspective, auditors must focus on the processes of the system rather than on outputs.

6. *Accountants must be consultants rather than gatekeepers.* Accountants at Lifeline Systems involve themselves early in the decision process to provide necessary financial guidance up front. This avoids unpleasant surprises at the time a decision is implemented. It appears that in many decision situations accountants can provide guidance on the resulting financial impact. These situations are as diverse as engineering changes (e.g., cost consequences of a part substitution) or repatriation of offshore operations (e.g., lower labor costs shown to be more than offset by logistics costs and reduced responsiveness). However, to be useful in these situations, accountants must understand the *prospective* financial impact of the decision and be able to communicate it effectively.

Conclusion

This Shingo Prize recipient appears to have effectively extended its Q^{10} philosophy throughout the organization. The accounting function, the focus of this study, has benefited from applying continuous improvement within a financial context. Among their accounting innovations are paperless purchasing, backflush cost transfers, activity-based costing, and direct deposit of travel reimbursement. In addition, accounting has provided important influence in such areas as product packaging, engineering changes, customer satisfaction measures, and measurement of the financial impact of the repatriation of offshore manufacturing operations.

References

Bogner, B. 1993. Supervisor, cost accounting, Lifeline Systems, Inc. On-site interview, May 13-14, 1993.

Bowdring, R.J. 1993. Controller, Lifeline Systems, Inc. On-site interview, May 13-14, 1993.

Dillon, J.M. 1993. Manager, production and manufacturing engineering, Lifeline Systems, Inc. On-site interview, May 13-14.

Giannetto, J. A. 1993. Corporate manager, materials and purchasing, Lifeline Systems, Inc. On-site interview, May 13-14.

Gugliotta, J. D. 1993. Vice president for operations, Lifeline Systems, Inc. On-site interview, May 13-14.

Gugliotta, J. D. 1991. Excellence Through Integration. Presented at the 1991 Quality and Productivity Conference, Utah State University, May.

10

The Shingo Management Accounting Profile

The experiences of eight Shingo Prize recipients provide a basis for developing a profile of lean management accounting. The following sections describe a composite set of characteristics typical of the Shingo environment.

The Integration of Business and Manufacturing Cultures

As explained in Chapter 1, the Shingo Prize is awarded to companies demonstrating that they not only have achieved a world-class level of competitiveness within their manufacturing operations but also have integrated quality management, waste reduction, and productivity enhancement methods throughout the organization. Service units such as accounting conduct themselves in much the same spirit as their manufacturing counterparts by decreasing their reporting cycle times, improving transaction processing accuracy, and eliminating unnecessary transaction processing and financial reporting. Not only do accountants in the lean manufacturing environment measure other departments, but they also scrutinize themselves, assuring through on-going measurement that accounting processes are producing quality output and that accounting responsibilities are being discharged effectively.

The Recognition of Lean Manufacturing and Its Effects on Management Accounting Measurements

The move from functional, batch-oriented manufacturing systems toward cellular, continuous-flow manufacturing has forced management accountants to reevaluate the methods used to measure the efficiency of productive capital utilization. Similarly, the tenacious focus of the Shingo Prize recipients on agile production methods (such as setup reduction) continues to shorten manufacturing cycle times and diminishes the justification for in-process transactions. These concepts are discussed more fully in the following sections.

■ Reduced Cycle Times

As manufacturing cycle times decline, the expenditure of human resources to record labor and material transactions as a product flows through its manufacturing processes would appear to make less sense. In many cases, the processing of such data lags significantly behind the physical flow of the product. A common practice in the Shingo environment is the use of backflushing, in which the resource consumption of a finished product is computed ex post facto using the bill of materials to relieve raw materials inventory and standard conversion times to apply burden to the product. As a result, production workers spend their time adding value to the product or improving processes, not recording transactions.

In addition to being a nonvalue-added activity on the production line, recording in-process transactions can actually create perverse incentives leading to local optimization. This is especially true when a functional department is measured by how much it transfers to a subsequent manufacturing process rather than by actual finished product shipments. For example, if a department can generate "revenue" or credit through transfers rather than customer shipments, it has the incentive to build excess inventory or perhaps to build assemblies that are easier to build and generate credit faster.

■ Cellular Manufacturing

The Shingo Prize recipients have recognized that the focus of efficiency measures should be at the manufacturing-cell level rather than at the machine or employee level. Clearly, the only meaningful utilization concern will be at each cell bottleneck; tracking the utilization of nonbottleneck resources is largely wasted effort.

■ Eliminating Accounting Barriers to Continuous Improvement

Traditionally, American management accounting measurements have focused on keeping labor fully utilized. The Japanese management style allows for time periods during which the worker is not physically engaged in production. This nonproduction time is expected to occur occasionally as pull-system demands have been met (i.e., the kanban is filled). Workers finding themselves in this situation use this time to pursue continuous improvement efforts rather than to build excess inventory.

Continuous Accounting Improvement

While management accounting is no stranger to scrutinizing other functional departments, it has a relatively short history of self-evaluation. Because companies within the Shingo environment have integrated continuous improvement methodologies throughout the organization, service departments such as accounting find themselves with the same continuous improvement mandate as the production departments.

The companies in this study show a variety of efforts aimed at continuous improvement. Some have involved the reduction in cycle times for reporting and month-end closing. Others have involved cause-and-effect analyses of credit memorandums and other transaction errors. Many of the companies were partnering actively with outside firms to reduce the complexity of transaction processing, the volume of paper document handling, and the resulting transaction costs. Most of the firms were actively pursuing mistake proofing of accounting processes. Also, metrics such as response time were used to measure and improve performance of the accounting function in returning bid quotations to customers.

The Elimination of Accounting Waste

Chapter 1 describes the seven types of waste targeted by Shigeo Shingo for elimination from the manufacturing process. A similar taxonomy of accounting wastes is compiled in the following sections.

■ Unnecessary Transaction Processing

Accountants understand the costs of transaction processing and should continually seek to eliminate those that do not lead to better decision making and organizational efficiency. The chart of accounts can be streamlined to reduce the time spent in account lookup and selection, minimize the chances for coding errors, and minimize computer storage and processing time. Accountants should also reduce the time spent on immaterial adjusting entries or unnecessary precision of accounting estimates—particularly if the adjustments cause delays in the closing and reporting process.

The Shingo Prize recipients have shown that travel expense transaction processing can be simplified through automation and reduced paper documentation processing. These firms also have shown that invoices can be consolidated and arrangements can be made with vendors to reduce the number of checks that need to be processed.

■ Processing Paper Documents

Clearly, handling paper documents results in several wasted actions and resources. These documents must be manually filed and retrieved, resulting in the waste of human effort and storage space. The documents must be physically routed, requiring additional time delays and misplaced documents. Paper documents require human action and are therefore subject to wait time in the "in" basket, making them less accessible and difficult to track.

Modern technology such as electronic data interchange (EDI) and electronic imaging should be explored aggressively as alternatives to paper handling.

■ Unnecessary Reports

Accountants need to determine the extent to which their products are being used. Accounting resources spent producing unused reports can be redeployed in other proactive efforts.

■ Unnecessary Controls and Procedures

The accounting profession must continue to reevaluate the appropriateness and cost effectiveness of controls and procedures. This reevaluation can be done without sacrificing prudence. For example, Iomega Corporation discontinued asset tagging because the fixed asset system already tracked capital purchases and associated serial numbers. United Electric reduced the number of employees in the authorization loop with respect to resolving small account discrepancies.

■ Accounting Artifacts

The term "artifact" often refers to a tool of an earlier civilization. Although such ancient tools at one time provided practical benefits to their users, these items are only curiosities today, rendered obsolete long ago by advancing technology. Similarly, some accounting procedures are rapidly becoming artifacts. For example, closing a plant or business to take a complete physical inventory is an artifact of an earlier era, before automated perpetual inventory and cycle counting. As the reliability of such modern systems becomes generally established, accountants can

The Shingo Management Accounting Profile

develop the expertise to audit and trust the systems rather than their outputs. The same can be said about any accounting procedure that forces the productive resources of the company to work around it.

■ Historical Analysis

Not surprisingly, production management finds little relevance in most historical reporting. For example, Dana Corporation has strictly limited backward-looking analyses. A more productive use of accounting resources may be to study the linkage of production processes to financial results, thus giving managers a forward-looking financial tool.

Toward a Proactive Management Accounting Culture

The preceding sections may seem to suggest that the management accounting role will diminish as a result of new technologies and a tenacious focus on eliminating nonvalue-added activities. While this view is probably a fair assessment of traditional management accounting activities, it overlooks the great need of the modern manufacturing plant for a proactive financial consultant. Interviews by the authors, both inside and outside the accounting function, suggest that management accounting has a significant opportunity to satisfy this need.

■ Becoming Business Consultants

Sentiments across the Shingo horizon are that manufacturing personnel would like to see less of the accountant in the role of a financial dictator, watchdog, or gatekeeper. What they do want is a financial advisor to help them run their businesses. It is also clear that manufacturing would like to see increased emphasis by accountants on future-oriented support and decreased emphasis on historical analyses. Areas such as strategic planning, up-front system design, and up-front product design offer important consulting opportunities for the management accounting profession.

■ Management Accounting Support That Empowers

Within the Shingo culture, it is at the level of the manufacturing cell that empowerment is taking root. Cells need to be able to develop measures for tracking their own performance. They are likely to need the assistance of the management accounting function in developing these measures. Management accounting is also in an excellent position to show the manufacturing cells how to access relevant data from the database.

■ Knowing the Core Business

The proactive involvement of the management accountant will require that he or she fully understand the core business and the production processes that drive it. As the Shingo companies have shown, management accountants need to be more directly involved with the production floor. This involvement will take several forms, such as cross-training, physical placement within production, job enrichment, and team participation. Clearly, the credibility of management accounting products will hinge directly on the degree to which management accountants are perceived as understanding the business and its operating processes.

■ Management Accountants as Educators

This study of eight Shingo Prize manufacturers reveals that management accounting must develop its role as the financial educator to the organization. Management accounting should strive to raise the level of financial understanding and sophistication of its audience. Management accounting is in the best position to study and articulate the linkages between operational measures and their corresponding financial results. These linkages will allow decision makers to evaluate prospective decisions and take them beyond postmortem analyses. Engineers will better understand the financial consequences of their design decisions. Finally, workers will better understand the financial consequences of their work patterns.

Appendices

Appendix 1: Research Methodology

The Methodology

Kaplan (1993) suggests that a field study approach involving firms with "considerable experience with the new practices" may yield promising results for the discipline of management accounting. He cautions, however, that because no "Japan" existed to serve as a laboratory for management accounting practices, field research studies would tend to "capture traditional management accounting systems operating in environments radically different from the ones for which the system was designed." Nevertheless, the authors of this manuscript assert that this field study offers a unique opportunity to capture a cross section of companies that have demonstrated world-class manufacturing prowess.

■ Setting for the Field Study

The Shingo Prize for Excellence in Manufacturing recognizes companies that have demonstrated excellence in manufacturing leading to enhanced product quality, increased productivity, and customer satisfaction. Named after the late Japanese manufacturing consultant Shigeo Shingo, the prize was established to facilitate enhanced awareness of lean, just-in-time manufacturing methodologies, foster the understanding and subsequent sharing of successful production methods, and encourage research in the areas of manufacturing processes and production improvement (Shingo Prize Council 1993). Eight companies agreed to participate in the study.

■ The Advance Questionnaire

An advance questionnaire was sent to each company to help them prepare for the types of questions to be asked in the site interviews. The questionnaire is reproduced in Appendix 2. The questionnaire was designed to elicit anecdotes and other documentation of the companies' experiences. Part I of the questionnaire asked each company to describe the role played by the management accounting function in the evolution of the organization toward world-class manufacturing. Part II asked the companies to identify the major functional areas now served by the management accounting function in the organization. Part III was designed to document the various operating activities presently supported by management accountants. Part IV asked the companies about the changes noted in their management accounting function as a result of changes in the manufacturing environment. In this section, they also were asked to suggest changes that ought to be made in the management accounting area. Finally, in Part V of the questionnaire, the companies were asked to document any innovative management accounting applications they have developed.

■ Site Visits to Participating Companies

The researchers conducted visits to the eight participating companies from March through June 1993. Key personnel were identified within each firm for the purpose of conducting site visit interviews. An attempt was made to examine various perspectives both inside and outside the management accounting function. The subjects typically included the plant manager, production foreman, procurement manager, engineering manager, chief financial officer, and cost accountants. The site visits were documented with the advance questionnaire, researchers' notes, and tape recordings of interview proceedings for later transcription.

■ Transcription, Editing, and Review

The researchers compiled individual site visit reports for each of the participating companies from tape recordings and notes. When complete, the reports were sent to the participating companies for editorial review. The research team then incorporated any necessary editorial changes into the chapters contained within this volume.

References

Kaplan, R.S. 1993. "Research opportunities in management accounting." *Journal of Management Accounting Research*, 5, Fall 1993, pp. 1-14.

Shingo Prize Council. 1993. *The Shingo Prize for Excellence in Manufacturing: 1993-94 application guidelines.*

2

Management Accounting in Support of Manufacturing Excellence Profiles of Award-Winning Organizations

Appendix 2: Advance Questionnaire and Site-Visit Discussion Guide

The research team sincerely appreciates the participation of the Shingo Prize recipients in this important study of manufacturing excellence and its implications for the management accounting function. We congratulate your organization for the success it has attained in achieving world-class stature in manufacturing. We also acknowledge the support of the distinguished sponsors of this endeavor: the *Institute of Management Accountants*, the *Utah State University Office of Research*, the *Office of Business Relations at the Utah State University College of Business,* and the *Utah State University School of Accountancy*.

The purpose of the Advance Questionnaire and Site-Visit Discussion Guide is to notify the participating organizations in advance of the areas of interest to the research team. This advance notification will allow the organization to determine the appropriate personnel to involve in the study, to gather appropriate documentation, and to formulate questionnaire responses.

You will note that the questions invite open-ended responses. The researchers strongly encourage the participating organizations to provide stories, anecdotes, histories, successes, failures, etc., to help the researchers put into perspective the evolution of the management accounting function. During the subsequent site visits by the research team, questionnaire responses and supporting materials will be reviewed and organized during interviews with the appropriate managers. The site visits will also provide an opportunity for researchers and participants to clarify questions and responses.

Because this questionnaire often uses the term management accounting, we define it as follows:

Management accounting: The portion of the accounting information system designated for the internal use of the organization. This would include, but not be limited to, accounting for the costs of products and services as well as providing other information (financial or nonfinancial) in support of decision makers within the organization.

The Questionnaire

■ Part I. Management Accounting Roles in Your Organization

(a) What role has the management accounting function played in the evolution of your organization toward world-class manufacturing? (Please include or attach such documentation as stories, anecdotes, and histories to describe either successes or failures in this area.)

(b) What role has management accounting played in the implementation of modern manufacturing techniques and management approaches? For example, has the management accounting function assumed important roles in implementing such programs as total quality management (TQM)? Have they been involved in just-in-time (JIT) manufacturing, or activity-based costing (ABC)? Has the management accounting function helped develop applications to support such new approaches? If so, please provide examples, anecdotes, etc., to illustrate your response.

■ Part II. Functional Areas Supported by Management Accounting

Please help us identify the major functional areas now served by the management accounting function in your organization. Please indicate briefly the type of support provided (information support applications) in the following areas:

(a) top management

(b) production management

Appendix 2

(c) quality control

(d) product engineering

(e) marketing

(f) other functional areas

■ Part III. Operating Activities Supported by Management Accounting

An important objective of this research project is to determine how management accountants are presently deployed in your organization. Would you please indicate which of the following operating activities are presently supported by management accountants? If such activities are supported by departments other than management accounting, please indicate the parties who support these activities. We would appreciate your including any additional examples, anecdotes, etc., that you feel would clarify your answers.

(a) measuring production costs

(b) controlling production costs

(c) measuring productivity

(d) improving production processes

(e) measuring customer satisfaction

(f) measuring product quality

(g) motivating employees

(h) monitoring key production activities

(i) measuring unused production capacity

(j) other activities supported (not included in sections a-i).

■ Part IV. The Evolution of the Management Accounting Function

(a) What changes have you noted in your management accounting function as a result of changes in your manufacturing environment? What changes have occurred in the way the management accounting function is organized? We would appreciate any examples, anecdotes, histories, etc., to illustrate your response.

(b) What changes ought to be made in the way management accounting performs its functions to support future information needs of the organization?

■ Part V. Innovative Management Accounting Applications

Please describe any innovative management accounting applications developed to support the operating activities of your organization. (The research team would be very interested in a demonstration or walk-through of such applications at the time of the site visit.)

The IMA Foundation for Applied Research, Inc.
Trustees, 1995-96

Foundation Officers

President
Robert C. Miller
The Boeing Company
Seattle, Washington

Treasurer
Joseph G. Harris
IMA Vice President
of Finance
The Upjohn Company
Kalamazoo, Michigan

Secretary
Gary M. Scopes, CAE
IMA Executive Director
Institute of Management
Accountants
Montvale, New Jersey

Trustees by Virtue of the Bylaws

Keith Bryant, Jr., CMA
IMA Chair
University of Alabama
   at Birmingham
Birmingham, Alabama

Joseph G. Harris
IMA Vice President of Finance
The Upjohn Company
Kalamazoo, Michigan

William J. Ihlanfeldt, CPA
IMA President
Formerly with Shell Oil Company
Houston, Texas

Frank C. Minter, CPA
IMA Vice President of Professional
   Relations
Samford University
Birmingham, Alabama

Clair M. Raubenstine, CMA, CPA
IMA President-elect
Coopers & Lybrand, LLP
Wayne, Pennsylvania

Gary M. Scopes, CAE
IMA Executive Director
Institute of Management Accountants
Montvale, New Jersey

Appointed Trustees

Victor Brown, CPA
George Mason University
Fairfax, Virginia

Paul P. Danesi, Jr.
Texas Instruments, Inc.
Attleboro, Massachusetts

Henry J. Davis, CMA, CPA
Reliance Electric Company
Greenville, South Carolina

Lou Jones
Caterpillar Company
Peoria, Illinois

Robert J. Melby
Defense Contract Audit Agency
Smyrna, Georgia

Kenneth A. Merchant, CPA
University of Southern California
Los Angeles, California

Robert C. Miller
The Boeing Company
Seattle, Washington

Milton Usry
University of West Florida
Pensacola, Florida

Robert C. Young
Digital Equipment Corporation
Nashua, New Hampshire

FAR Publications Available

Management Accounting Issues in Cellular Manufacturing and Focused-Factory Systems, by Dileep G. Dhavale   96310/$60

This book provides background material, basic concepts, and methods for developing a cellular manufacturing system. Information in the book is based on current industry practices.

The Theory of Constraints and Its Implications for Management Accounting, by Eric Noreen, Debra Smith, and James T. Mackey   95300/$40

The theory of constraints has profound implications for the way cost and financial reporting systems and management controls are constructed. The authors visited sites that had put the theory of constraints into practice. The book contains detailed case studies of seven of these companies.

Measuring Corporate Environmental Performance: Best Practices for Costing and Managing an Effective Environmental Strategy,
by Marc J. Epstein   95301/$40

The author surveyed the management of a number of large organizations to discover how environmental costs and strategies affect decision making. He suggests ways to incorporate good environmental practices into an organization's overall management strategy.

Expert Systems for Management Accounting Tasks, by Carol E. Brown and Mary Ellen Phillips   94299/$40

This study describes the types of tasks suitable for solution with expert-system technology and relates those tasks to specific managerial accounting problems.

IMA's Legacy: Creating Value Through Research, by Patrick L. Romano
          95305/$20

This annotated bibliography of all the research monographs published by the IMA since its founding (as the National Association of Cost Accountants) gives a comprehensive view of the wide range of subjects covered by that research.

FAR's 1996/97 Publications Catalog lists 59 titles and all IMA's Statements on Management Accounting. A copy of the catalog is available upon request.

Call IMA's Special Orders Department, 1-800-638-4427, ext. 278.